THE
MIRACLE OF
CIDER VINEGAR

Dr Penny Stanway practised for several years as a GP and as a child-health doctor before becoming increasingly fascinated in researching and writing about a healthy diet and other natural approaches to health and wellbeing. She is an accomplished cook who loves eating and very much enjoys being creative in the kitchen and sharing food with others. Penny has written more than 20 books on health, food, and the connections between the two. She lives with her husband in a houseboat on the Thames and often visits the south-west of Ireland. Her leisure pursuits include painting, swimming and being with her family and friends.

THE
MIRACLE OF
CIDER VINEGAR

Practical Tips for Home & Health

DR PENNY STANWAY

WATKINS PUBLISHING

LONDON

This edition published in the UK 2010 by
Watkins Publishing, Sixth Floor, Castle House,
75–76 Wells Street, London W1T 3QH

3 5 7 9 10 8 6 4

Designed and typeset by Paul Saunders
Printed and bound in China

British Library Cataloguing-in-Publication data available

ISBN: 978-1-906787-64-6

www.watkinspublishing.co.uk

*In memory of John Rench, my much-loved father,
who particularly enjoyed vinegar on cockles
and soft herring roe.*

Contents

Acknowledgements

Thank you to my sister, Jenny Hare, for sharing my passion for food and cooking; to my husband, Andrew, for his unstinting enthusiasm in discussing apples and cider vinegar; and to my agent, Doreen Montgomery, for her endless encouragement and support.

Introduction

Apples are the most popular fruit in the world, and I certainly love eating them! I also enjoy drinking apple juice and cider, and cooking with cider vinegar, so writing this book has been an ongoing source of fascination to me. Creating and testing the recipes has been a pleasure, and I remain amazed and intrigued by the myriad ways in which apples, apple juice, cider and cider vinegar can benefit our health.

I grew up in a nursing home run by my parents. My mother, a nursing sister, used to say, 'An apple a day keeps the doctor away', and there were always apples for us to eat. Now, after my many years of experience of being a doctor and of researching health matters as a medical writer, I am even more certain that apples and cider vinegar are able to promote and protect our health and wellbeing. What's more, cider vinegar is a cheap and efficient source of help in the home.

Archaeologists believe that apple trees originated around the Caspian Sea and the Black Sea, and that people ate apples as far back as 6500 BC. Apple cultivation spread to Europe and in the 16th century King Henry VIII instructed his fruiterer to search the world for the best varieties, so he could set up orchards in England. Apple cultivation spread to the US, Australia, New Zealand, South Africa and South America. Nowadays, more than 7,500 varieties of apple are grown world-wide, and in many countries either home-grown or imported apples are available year-round.

Historians are unsure when people first enjoyed cider, but they know it was a common drink in Britain in the first century BC and think it was probably available around the Mediterranean in the 1st century AD. In contrast, archaeol-ogists say that cider vinegar has been used for much longer, since traces of it exist in Egyptian urns dating from 3000 BC.

Apples, apple juice, cider and cider vinegar have a long history and are much loved around the world. In *The Miracle of Cider Vinegar* I'll explain their surprising properties and valuable uses, and I hope you'll agree that it's a really good idea to use cider vinegar and have at least one apple every day.

A short note

- What the English call 'apple juice' is known as 'cider' or 'sweet cider' in some countries, including the US.

- What the English call 'cider' is called 'hard cider' in some countries, including the US.

CHAPTER ONE

What's in Apples, Apple Juice, Cider and Cider Vinegar

Apples

When you eat an apple, you aren't just getting a sugary source of 50 calories with some fibre and vitamin C. You are consuming a veritable treasure chest of health-promoting substances, some of which occur in such richness in only a few other foods. For example, apples are one of the most plentiful sources of pectin fibre and phenolic compounds such as quercetin. This explains why apples are the fruits most consistently associated with a reduced risk of certain chronic diseases, including heart disease, cancer, and diabetes, and why consuming apples, apple juice and cider vinegar really can make a difference to our health and wellbeing.

Major nutrients

Apples are rich in fibre and sugars – including fructose, sucrose, glucose, oligosaccharides and inulin (not insulin!). An unripe apple's carbohydrate is mainly starch, but ripening converts most of this to sugars. Apples also contain useful amounts of vitamin C and potassium. A medium-size (100g or 3½oz) apple, for example, supplies 8 per cent of the vitamin C and 10 per cent of the potassium the average adult needs each day.

Certainly apples contain extremely little fat and protein and only very small amounts of beta-carotene, B vitamins, calcium, iron, magnesium, phosphorus and zinc. But even these small amounts contribute to our necessary daily intake. The tiny amounts of trace elements such as boron and chromium are useful too. Boron, for example, is critical to the way the body uses calcium and may help prevent the bone loss of osteoporosis. It also affects the release, use and lifespan of steroid hormones.

Fibre

Dietary fibre, once called roughage, is now officially known as non-starch polysaccharides. I'll call it fibre, though it often isn't fibrous!

Not only do apples contain cellulose, hemi-cellulose and the non-carbohydrate fibre lignin but they are also a rich source of pectin. Indeed, pectin forms 70 per cent of apple fibre and apples are richer in pectin than are any other fruits. Cellulose strengthens plant cell walls; pectin helps hold these together. Both benefit health in different ways. As water-insoluble types of fibre, cellulose and lignin passively absorb water in the digestive tract but pass through unchanged. As a water-soluble type of fibre, pectin dissolves in water in the digestive tract to form a gel. About 90 per cent of the pectin in this gel is fermented by the 'good' bacteria in the large intestine, releasing valuable short-chain fatty acids such as butyric acid, and aiding the absorption of calcium and other minerals.

Unfortunately, many people don't get enough fibre in their diet. In the US, for example, the average intake is only half what it should be.

One medium apple provides more than 10 per cent of our daily recommended fibre intake. More than half the health-promoting fibre is in the peel and core, so it's best to eat an apple unpeeled – core and all. The perfect apple is firm, crisp and not overripe. The riper an apple becomes, the softer and mealier it is and the less pectin it contains. 'Cooking' apples are green and tart even when ripe, and are good for stewing, baking and apple pies, because heat makes their pectin soft and mushy. The peel of both cooking and dessert apples, though, remains largely intact on cooking, because its cell walls are particularly rich in insoluble fibre.

Antioxidants

Antioxidants are substances that help prevent uncontrolled oxidation. Oxidation is a chemical reaction caused by free radicals (overactive oxygen particles); it is involved in many of the body's normal metabolic processes. Certain circumstances, such as a poor diet, infection, smoking and stress, increase the production of free radicals, which can lead to a chain reaction of oxidation. This uncontrolled oxidation can encourage problems such as inflammation, infection, cancer, premature ageing, heart attacks and strokes.

Apples are a good source of antioxidants. Much of an apple's antioxidant content is in its peel, which is another reason to eat apples unpeeled. Apple antioxidants include vitamin C and various phenolic compounds (such as quercetin and phlorizin), plus tiny amounts of selenium and zinc. An apple contains one-and-a-half times more antioxidant capacity than 75g of blueberries, more than twice that of a cup of tea, three times that of an orange and almost eight times that of a banana.

Scientists from Cornell University in New York have found that a 100g (4oz) apple is as powerful an antioxidant as 1,500mg of vitamin C. So, given that such an apple contains only about 5.7mg of vitamin C, most of its antioxidant activity must come from other compounds. An apple's antioxidant power is greatest if eaten whole and raw soon after picking and otherwise stored in a cold dark place such as a fridge.

Phenolic compounds

This is an umbrella term for a group of apple phytochemicals that includes flavonoids, various acids, tannins and lignins (a non-carbohydrate type of fibre). These are all derived from phenolic acid and are sometimes called polyphenols or phenolics. Their level in apples varies from year to year, variety to variety, tree to tree, and region to region. Apple peel contains up to six times more than apple flesh. Apples are the major source of dietary phenolic compounds in many parts of the world, including the US and Europe.

Apples are particularly rich in flavonoids, the most abundant of which are quercetin and other flavonols. Quercetin has antioxidant, antihistamine and anti-inflammatory actions. It is found almost only in peel, and red apples contain more than do green or yellow ones. Quercetin is relatively stable when apples are cooked.

Other apple flavonoids include proanthocyanidins (such as the plant pigment catechin which contributes colour to peel and astringency and bitterness to an apple's flavour); phlorizin; and the plant hormone genistein (*see* below).

An apple's phenolic acids include chlorogenic acid, p-coumaric and quinic acids. Tannins help account for any astringent flavour, and the oxidation of tannins in cut apples is responsible for their subsequent brown discolouration.

Plant hormones (phytosterols)

Apples contain very small amounts of the flavonoid genistein, which is a phyto-oestrogen (plant oestrogen) and an antioxidant. The amount in an apple is tiny, but nevertheless contributes to an individual's overall phyto-oestrogen intake. By latching on to oestrogen receptors on cells, phyto-oestrogens have an oestrogen-balancing action. If a woman is making unusually large amounts of her own, stronger oestrogen, the occupation of cell receptors by weaker phyto-oestrogens prevents her oestrogen encouraging problems associated with oestrogen dominance (such as heavy periods). If she isn't making enough oestrogen, the occupation of cell receptors by phyto-oestrogens provides some small oestrogenic stimulation which can aid conditions associated with oestrogen deficiency (such as hot flushes).

Organic acids

These include malic and tartaric acids. The amount of malic acid in each variety helps determine its tartness. The more malic acid and the less sugar an apple contains, the stronger its flavour and the greater its likelihood of retaining flavour when cooked. Unripe apples and cooking apples contain more malic acid than do other apples.

Wax and pesticides

Apple skin is coated in natural protective wax produced by the apple. Washing apples with water removes about half of this, so some commercial growers coat their produce with an officially approved edible wax (such as carnauba or shellac) to make them shiny and help prevent desiccation and rotting.

Apples may have pesticide residues on their peel. The levels are monitored and should be safe. However, many people prefer to wash an apple with water before eating or cooking it. This removes added waxes and pesticides.

Pips

Apple pips taste slightly bitter and almond-like, due to a small amount of a substance called amygdalin. This can be converted to poisonous cyanide by an enzyme that is present in a few of the body's cells, though abundant in cancer cells. Eating a few apples complete with pips each day is highly unlikely to pose a problem and it might (though this is unproven) act against early cancer cells.

Apple scent and flavour

An apple's scent and flavour result from its particular blend of about 250 volatile compounds, which include various esters (such as ethyl-methyl-butyrate, isobutyl acetate), alcohols, aldehydes and essential oils. The aroma and flavour of some unusual varieties resemble those of melon, strawberry, raspberry, peach, lemon, fennel, cinnamon, allspice, banana or pineapple.

Apple colour

This colour comes from traces of chlorophyll (a green pigment), carotenoids (yellow and orange pigments) and proanthocyanidins (pigments of various hues). Red-skinned apples tend to be sweet, green ones may be tart or sweet.

Apple Juice

Apple juice is called 'apple cider' in the US and parts of Canada. Apple juice diluted with water, or sweetened with added sugar, must be labelled as an 'apple drink' or 'apple-juice beverage'. Juicing apples requires mechanical pressing, which produces cloudy juice.

Other possible processes include:

- Filtering of particulate material, including cellulose, pectins and proteins. This produces clear juice.

- Pasteurization, to prevent enzymes turning sugars to alcohols, and to protect against the growth of moulds and bacteria. This gives the juice a shelf life of up to two years. Unpasteurized juice should ideally be consumed as soon as possible.

The less processing there is, the smaller the loss of nutrients and other valuable phytochemicals. Cloudy (unfiltered) juice is slightly richer in fibre than is clear (filtered) juice. It is also much richer in valuable phenolic compounds, containing, for example, a much higher amount of proanthocyanidins. And while it contains around half the amount of phenolic compounds of apples themselves, clear juice contains only up to a third or so.

Cider

Cider is an alcoholic beverage made by the fermentation of apple juice. In the US, any fermented apple juice containing more than 0.5 per cent ABV (alcohol by volume, meaning millilitres of alcohol per 100 millilitres of liquid) is called 'hard cider'. In the UK, 1.2 per cent ABV cider is designated 'low-alcohol' cider. More often, the alcohol content of cider varies from less than 3 per cent ABV (for example, French *cidre doux*) to 8.5 per cent ABV or more (for example, in traditional English ciders).

The flavour of ciders differs according to the apples or blends of apples used. Their colour varies from very pale gold ('white cider') to rich golden brown. The trend today is to make cider from a single crop of a single apple variety. The flavour of such a cider reflects the particular blend of volatile phytochemicals in that variety of apple; the cider can also be sold as being of a defined 'vintage'. You can use any apples to make cider; however, many cider makers like to include cider apples in their chosen blend. This is because these contain higher levels of tannins and more malic acid and other organic acids than do sweet 'dessert' apples, and give cider a characteristic 'bite'.

Cider apples are grouped in four categories according to their flavour components:

Bittersweets are high in sugar, which raises the cider's alcohol content. They are also relatively high in tannins, so the cider is quite bitter.

Bittersharps are high in tannins and fruit acids (for example, malic acid), so the cider is relatively bitter and sharp.

Sweets are high in sugar, which raises the cider's alcohol. They are low in tannins and fruit acid, so the cider has little bitterness or sharpness.

Sharps are high in acidity, which adds sharpness to their cider. They are low in sugar and tannins, so the cider is a little less alcoholic or bitter.

Cider's nutritional content relates to that of the apple juice from which it came, the type of fermentation, and any extra processing (such as filtration or pasteurization). Cloudy cider has a higher concentration of pectin and phenolic compounds than clear cider. For example, clear cider may have only 1–5 per cent of the proanthocyanidin content of cloudy cider.

Cider contains relatively high levels of antioxidants: indeed, half a pint contains the same amount as a glass of red wine.

Lastly, cider contains fermentation products such as alcohol (derived from the apples' sugar) and small amounts of lactic acid (derived from the apples' malic acid, and which can add an interesting flavour). Cider is increasingly fashionable, but, however enjoyable it may be, it's wise to keep your alcohol intake within recommended limits.

Making cider

To make cider, cloudy or clear apple juice is either left to ferment naturally, or wine yeast is added to speed fermentation and make it more reliable. Shortly before fermentation ceases, the cider is siphoned off, leaving a sediment of dead yeast cells and other material at the bottom of the container. This is called 'racking from the lees'. Sparkling cider is made by allowing fermentation of the remaining sugar and, perhaps, adding more.

Most commercially produced cider is also treated in other ways. It is usually pasteurized – heated to 71°C (160°F) or treated with ultraviolet light to kill bacteria and moulds. Unpasteurized cider can be risky for pregnant women, young children and people with poor immunity. But while pasteurization renders cider safer and increases shelf life, it can slightly alter its flavour. It also destroys enzymes and inhibits oxidation, giving a less distinct flavour.

What's more, much commercial cider is made from apple concentrate, contains artificial colourings, sweeteners, preservatives and enzymes, and is filtered. It may have a source of nitrogen added and be stored under compressed carbon dioxide gas. All this makes cider production more reliable and changes the colour, clarity and flavour of cider in ways some people prefer. Others prefer the appearance and flavour of simply made 'natural' or 'real' cider.

The UK's Apple and Pear Produce Liaison Executive (APPLE) aims to encourage appreciation of 'real' cider. They say top quality real cider must:

- be produced only from freshly pressed fruit

- not contain concentrate

- not be diluted

- not be pasteurized before or after fermentation

- not be fermented by added yeast

- not be treated with an enzyme

- not contain preservatives or colouring

- only contain sweeteners if labelled 'medium' or 'sweet', and then only if the sweetener is provably safe and does not affect the flavour

- not be filtered

- not have a nitrogen source added unless essential to start fermentation

- not be exposed to extraneous carbon dioxide

Scrumpy can mean cider made from scrumps – or windfalls. Or it can mean cloudy and unsophisticated cider. Or it can mean 'young' cider of a few months old that has not undergone maturation (which includes malolactic fermentation converting malic acid into lactic acid). Or it can mean fine cider made from choice apples, slowly fermented and matured longer than ordinary cider.

Apple Wine is usually made from dessert apples, so lacks sharpness ('bite', from fruit acid) and bitterness (from tannins). It often contains a higher concentration of alcohol too. The alcohol content of cider is nearly always less than 8 per cent ABV, whereas apple wine is usually more alcoholic.

Cider Vinegar

Making cider vinegar involves two basic types of fermentation. First, the sugars of apple juice are fermented to the alcohol of cider. Then the alcohol of cider is fermented to the acetic acid of cider vinegar (a process sometimes called 'acetification').

The colour of cider vinegar is a light brownish-yellow. It can be cloudy or clear. It can also be pasteurized (in which case it contains no microorganisms) or unpasteurized (in which case it contains some of the cloudy mass of fermentation bacteria called the 'vinegar mother').

Cider vinegar is not a rich source of nutrients. One table-spoon, for example, contains a little carbohydrate, very small amounts of minerals, extremely tiny amounts of trace elements, and virtually no protein, fat, vitamins or fibre. Some people claim it's a good source of calcium, but it isn't. We need around 1,000mg of calcium a day from food. One tablespoon of cider vinegar contains only 1mg, whereas one tablespoon of milk contains 20mg. There is a paradox here, though, because many people, including around one in two over-60s, make insufficient stomach acid for optimal absorption of calcium and certain other minerals. Cider vinegar can increase stomach acidity for such people, in which case it increases the absorption of calcium from foods.

Cider vinegar has many health-giving properties. Many come from its organic acids (such as acetic and lactic acids and, perhaps, traces of malic acid). These acids are mainly responsible for its antifungal, antibacterial and antiviral actions. Malic acid, the main organic acid in apple juice, is fermented to milder lactic acid during alcoholic and acetic fermentation. A by-product of this malolactic fermentation is a chemical with an attractive flavour that also contributes to the flavour of Chardonnay wine and the spread 'I Can't Believe It's Not Butter'. Most commercial cider vinegars contain 5 per cent acetic acid.

Cider vinegar adds to the stomach's natural acidity. It is absorbed from the gut into the bloodstream and almost completely oxidized in the body's cells to produce energy. Although it contains acids, its overall effect, once absorbed from the gut, is usually said to be slightly alkaline. Certain scientists explain this by saying that if vinegar is burnt in the laboratory to a dry ash, this is alkaline when tested with a pH (acid-alkaline) meter. They say the oxidation of vinegar's acids in cells to produce energy is equivalent to vinegar being burnt in the laboratory.

Good cider vinegar is aged slowly. Its flavour is enriched and its composition made more complex during fermentation and subsequent ageing by volatile compounds such as aldehydes, ketones, alcohols, ethyl acetates, enzymes, phenolic compounds, salicylates and carboxylic acids (such as acetic, malic, lactic and succinic acids).

Cider vinegar tablets may contain no cider vinegar at all! Instead they may contain weak organic acid salts and flavourings that make them smell vinegary.

CHAPTER TWO

Natural Remedies

The saying, 'An apple a day keeps the doctor away', is proving very true.

Fruit makes an invaluable contribution to good health. Researchers recommend at least five helpings of fruit and vegetables a day; two of every five can be fruit; and one of these two can be fruit juice. However, many people fail to get anywhere near five-a-day. A survey by TNS Worldpanel UK in 2008 found only 12 per cent of respondents had five-a-day, while 12 per cent had none.

Fruit is health-promoting and enjoyable, and apples are especially so. They are very rich in certain substances – for example, flavonoids and pectin – that have important health benefits. A research review (*Nutrition Journal*, 2004) found apples were more consistently associated with a reduced risk of cancer, diabetes and heart disease than any other fruit (or vegetable). Apple consumption was also linked with less asthma, better lung function and increased weight loss. While apple juice and cider are less rich in health-giving ingredients than apples, they have some value and are delicious to drink.

As for cider vinegar, reports of its healing properties date from thousands of years ago. In 400 BC, the Greek doctor Hippocrates used it as an antibiotic and for general health. Samurai warriors used a vinegar tonic for strength, and a vinegar solution was used to prevent stomach upsets and treat pneumonia and scurvy in the US Civil War and to treat wounds in World War I. But while traditional use, common sense and anecdotal evidence suggest cider vinegar can help a wide variety of ailments, few trials have been done. One reason is that it's difficult to get funding as cider vinegar can't be patented.

In this chapter I'll detail how and why apples, apple juice or cider vinegar might help, and whether this is based on traditional usage, anecdotal or medical evidence, or common sense.

Remember that you can also discourage common ailments with a healthy diet, adequate hydration, regular exercise, daily outdoor light, effective stress management, a sensible alcohol intake and no smoking.

Also, nothing should take the place of proper medical diagnosis and therapy. Check with your doctor before using cider vinegar with any existing medical treatment. And please bear in mind these side effects and safety issues:

- Anyone allergic to cider vinegar, apples or any apple constituent, such as pectin, should avoid them.

- The acidity of cider vinegar may temporarily soften tooth enamel, making it vulnerable to damage. So dilute it, use a straw, rinse your mouth with water afterwards, and don't clean your teeth immediately after.

- Excessive amounts of undiluted cider vinegar, or cider vinegar tablets, might damage the gullet and other parts of the digestive tract.

- Cider vinegar tablets may stick in the throat or gullet, so wash them down well.

- A study in the US in 2005 found the ingredients of eight brands of cider vinegar tablet did not correspond with the details on packaging; analysis made researchers query whether they really contained only acetic acid.

- Prolonged use of cider vinegar could theoretically lower potassium, which could encourage toxicity from certain drugs (for example, digoxin, insulin, laxatives and certain diuretics).

- Cider vinegar affects blood sugar and insulin, so might have an additive effect if combined with diabetes medication.

- Cider vinegar may lower blood pressure, so it might have an additive effect if it is combined with high blood pressure medication.

When I mention a study, I give the journal's name and year of publication; this plus some keywords should enable you to find out more via an Internet search engine.

Ailments and Remedies

Acne

One cause of acne is overproduction of sebum due to over-sensitivity of sebaceous glands to testosterone. Other possibilities are changes in sebum and unusually sticky hair-follicle cells. Other triggers include the premenstrual fall in oestrogen, humidity, stress, certain drugs (for example, the progestogen-only pill), and polycystic ovary syndrome. A reduction in the skin's normal acidity may encourage infected spots.

Some people report that cider vinegar helps; if so, it could be because it kills bacteria, increases skin acidity, 'cuts' (emulsifies) skin oil, and reduces inflammation.

Action: Mix 1 part of cider vinegar with 4 parts of water. Apply with cotton wool, rinse after 10 minutes and repeat three times a day.

Age spots

The most common are brown freckles ('liver spots'), caused by normal ageing plus photo-ageing (accelerated ageing from sun exposure).

Some people report that applying cider vinegar – particularly if mixed with onion juice – lightens age spots.

Action: Finely chop an onion, wrap it in muslin and squeeze to extract the juice. Mix 2 teaspoons of cider vinegar with 1 teaspoon of onion juice and apply the mixture to the freckles twice a day. They may begin to lighten within six weeks.

Ageing

Scientists have long searched for lifestyle factors that encourage long life and discourage age-related diseases (such as arthritis, heart disease, diabetes, cancer, osteoporosis and Alzheimer's). Long-lived peoples include certain groups in Russia (the Georgians), Pakistan (the Hunzas), Ecuador, China, Tibet and Peru. One link is that they tend to live at high altitudes; here, melting glacier water is rich in alkaline minerals such as calcium, which help the body maintain a healthy pH (acid-alkaline balance) without drawing calcium from the bones.

Apples, apple juice and cider vinegar have an alkalinizing effect in the body, so they, too, help conserve stored calcium.

Another possible factor encouraging these peoples' longevity is their consumption of fermented vegetables, fruit, milk, cereal grains, meat or fish. We don't yet know whether any benefit is caused by fermentation reducing the carbohydrate in the food; by any remaining fermentation bacteria; or by the presence of fermentation acids (such as lactic or acetic). Whatever the reason, folk medicine has long held that cider vinegar (fermented apple juice) helps protect against age-related disease; certainly, consuming it before a meal discourages high blood sugar afterwards (*see* Diabetes). Also, people with an age-related reduction in stomach acid (one in two over-60s in Westernized cultures) who take cider vinegar, aid their absorption of many nutrients (including protein, carbohydrates, fats, vitamins A, B, C and E, calcium, iron, magnesium, zinc, copper, chromium, selenium, manganese, vanadium, molybdenum, cobalt).

US researchers say mineral and vitamin deficiencies can accelerate the age-related decay of mitochondria (energy-providing structures in cells). Among the most important deficiencies are those of iron, zinc, biotin, pantothenic acid, magnesium and manganese.

Molecular Aspects of Medicine, 2005

Apples can help reduce inflammation associated with heart disease, arthritis and Alzheimer's, because they contain anti-oxidants and aspirin-like salicylates with anti-inflammatory actions. Unpeeled apples contain larger amounts. Apple juice contains smaller amounts.

Apple consumption is also associated with a reduced risk of cancer, strokes and type 2 diabetes (*see* Chronic Illness).

Lastly, pectin binds to potentially toxic heavy metals such as aluminium and lead in the gut, which encourages their elimination. Indeed, pectin is regularly prescribed in Russia to remove heavy metals from the body. Such metals can form damaging 'cross-links' with brain and other cells. So, pectin's binding ability may mean it helps protect against premature degeneration and ageing.

Action: Until we know more, hedge your bets by eating an apple a day, and either adding cider vinegar to various recipes, or taking 2 teaspoons in a glass of water 2 or 3 times a day.

Alzheimer's disease

This results from brain-cell destruction and is associated with patches of amyloid protein and clusters of tangled nerve fibres. The cause isn't clear, but it can run in families and is more likely with age and after a serious head injury.

It's possible, though unproven, that eating apples might help prevent Alzheimer's or slow its development. One reason is that people with Alzheimer's tend to have high levels of the amino acid homocysteine, and are particularly likely to lack those B vitamins that help normalize homocysteine levels. Apples contain small amounts of folic acid and vitamin B6, which are among the B vitamins with the greatest effect. So they can make a useful contribution to the intake of vitamin B.

Several studies suggest that a small daily dose of aspirin or other non-steroidal anti-inflammatory drug discourages Alzheimer's. There isn't enough evidence for doctors to recommend taking such drugs long-term, and they can make the stomach bleed. But unpeeled apples, and apple juice, cider and cider vinegar made from unpeeled apples, are good sources of salicylates with aspirin-like qualities.

What's more, research suggests that brain damage due to the oxidation of the fatty acids arachidonic acid and docosahexaenoic acid contributes to Alzheimer's – and apples contain antioxidants.

Finally, studies suggest that increasing the amount of a neurotransmitter (nerve-message carrier) called acetylcholine in the brain can slow the mental decline associated with Alzheimer's. More recent research suggests that apples, and apple juice in particular, may help by increasing acetylcholine levels.

Laboratory tests in the US and Korea found that the antioxidant plant pigment quercetin helps protect rat brain cells from oxidation. Apple peel is rich in quercetin. So it's possible that eating unpeeled apples may help prevent Alzheimer's.

Journal of Agricultural and Food Chemistry, 2004

Researchers at the University of Massachusetts suspect that nutrients in apples and apple juice improve memory in mice, and protect against the oxidative damage that contributes to age-related brain disorders such as Alzheimer's. Consuming apple juice protected the mice from oxidative stress and slightly improved memory, possibly by increasing acetylcholine in the brain.

Journal on Nutrition Health and Aging, 2004

Action: Eat an apple a day as this will benefit your general health and it might even help prevent Alzheimer's.

Anaemia

Iron-deficiency anaemia can be associated with low stomach acid, which affects one in two over-60s. It can also result from stress or the prolonged use of antacid or acid-suppressant medication. A lack of stomach acid can reduce iron absorption from food. Vitamin B12-deficiency anaemia is another possible result of low stomach acid.

Eating apples could be particularly useful if you have iron-deficiency anaemia. Gut bacteria break down apple pectin, releasing short-chain fatty acids which raise acidity and thereby boost iron absorption.

Action: If you have iron- or vitamin B12-deficiency anaemia, try improving your absorption of either nutrient by drinking a glass of water containing 2 teaspoons of cider vinegar in water before each meal, or by adding cider vinegar to a dressing for a first-course salad or soup.

Anxiety

Eating apples might help reduce anxiety and panic attacks.

Researchers found that the urine of people with panic attacks was unusually acidic. Kidneys produce unusually acidic urine to help keep the blood's pH (acid-alkaline balance) within normal limits. One reason for overly acidic urine is an unbalanced diet with insufficient vegetables and fruit.

Psychiatry Research, 2005

Action: Try eating more apples, other fruit, and vegetables for a month or so.

Arthritis

Inflammation links the many sorts of arthritis. Although some people claim that cider vinegar helps their arthritis, others say it doesn't. While it's certainly possible that people might react in different ways, there is no scientific evidence, so the jury remains out.

Apples could help reduce the inflammation that often accompanies arthritis, because they contain antioxidants (such as proanthocyanidin plant pigments, beta carotene, vitamin C, selenium) and aspirin-like salicylates.

Action: You may want to see if cider vinegar helps. Use it in salad dressings, soups or other recipes, or drink 2 teaspoons in a glass of water 3 times a day with meals.

A folk remedy for arthritis in the hands or feet is to soak them 3 times a day in a solution made by adding 1 cup of cider vinegar to 3 cups of hot water.

Eat apples unpeeled to get larger amounts of natural anti-inflammatories. Apple juice contains smaller amounts and the best choice is cloudy juice made from crushed whole apples.

Asthma

Inflammation and oversensitivity of airways causes wheezing, coughing and a tight chest. Possible triggers include cold air, exercise, certain foods, hormone changes, laughter, infection, various fumes, a sudden fall in air pressure, thunderstorms, allergy, and breathing too fast.

Apples and apple juice have an anti-asthma effect that seems stronger than that of any other food. This may result from their high levels of antioxidants such as quercetin, as these have a provable anti-inflammatory effect.

UK researchers reported that adults who ate at least two apples a week decreased their asthma risk by up to a third. They suggested that flavonoids in apples may be responsible.

American Journal of Respiratory Critical Care Medicine, 2001

Another study found no protective effect from 3 subclasses of flavonoids (catechins, flavonols and flavones), suggesting that protection is due to other flavonoids.

European Respiratory Journal, 2005

Children of mothers who eat apples in pregnancy are much less asthma-prone in the first five years, say UK researchers. They attributed this to phenolic acids and other flavonoids.

Thorax, 2007

A study of children with wheezing found that drinking apple juice once a day was associated with improvement.

European Respiratory Journal, 2007

As for cider vinegar, Dr DC Jarvis, who studied 24 people in the US over two years in the 1950s, found their urine pH became highly alkaline before and early on in an asthma attack (*Folk Medicine*). On following his suggestion to drink cider vinegar, their urine rapidly returned to its normal acid pH and the asthma attack was less severe. He attributed this to its organic acids and potassium content.

On searching for a clearer explanation, I came across a 1931 paper by Dr George W Bray of The Hospital for Sick Children, London. He measured stomach acid after a meal in more than 200 children with asthma. Astonishingly, 9 per cent had no stomach acid, 48 per cent had a severe lack, and 23 per cent a slight lack. So 80 per cent had an absence or deficiency of stomach acid. Other researchers have found a lack of stomach acid in many adults with asthma, as well as in people with other allergic conditions, including eczema, urticaria and hay fever. Dr Bray also found that the blood of children with asthma was unusually alkaline. He suggested that their body's acid-producing ability was reducing the alkalinity of their blood instead of making stomach acid. He quotes an earlier study (*Journal of Physiology* 1926–7) which suggests that sudden repeated exposure of sensitized tissue to a slight increase in alkalinity is extremely effective in triggering an exaggerated response. This implies that unusual alkalinity of blood and tissue fluid makes sensitized lung-lining cells more likely to become inflamed.

One possible cause of allergic sensitization is absorption

from the gut of poorly digested protein, associated with low stomach acid. This work is extraordinarily interesting but has been largely ignored.

Action: Taking cider vinegar can restore some acidity to the stomach in someone with low levels of their own stomach acid. If you suspect this (for example, because you get indigestion that is not relieved by antacid medication), you might want to try taking cider vinegar either regularly each day to help prevent asthma, or early in an attack to help cure it.

For an adult, put 1 tablespoon of cider vinegar into a glass of water and sip over half an hour. Wait another half-hour then repeat. Or put 1 tablespoon of cider vinegar in soup or salad dressing. For children, use less cider vinegar, depending on their size.

Athlete's foot

This fungal infection makes the skin between the toes sore and soggy, and is often picked up in changing rooms or around swimming pools. Anecdotal reports suggest cider vinegar might help.

Action: Each day bathe your feet for 5–10 minutes in warm water containing 4 tablespoons of cider vinegar and 10 drops of tea tree oil.

Bronchitis and emphysema

These two types of chronic obstructive lung disease often require ever more intensive treatment. Studies suggest apples may help. Most researchers believe that antioxidants are protective, and some think the flavonol quercetin plays a key role. Other constituents that may help include other flavonoids, pectins and malic acid.

A London study of 2,512 men found apples were the only food to benefit lung function. Volunteers eating five a week had a lung capacity 138ml (nearly ¼ pint, or up to 3 per cent) higher than those eating none. This extra volume could make a big difference to 'puffability'. Apples seemed to slow the deterioration associated with smoking, and the authors thought that flavonoid antioxidants such as quercetin might be responsible.

Thorax, 2000

Researchers at the University of Nottingham found less respiratory diseases in apple eaters.

Thoracic Society, annual meeting 2001

Action: Eat an apple a day as this will benefit your general health and as studies suggest it might help prevent or ease bronchitis or emphysema.

Bruises

These are associated with leaking of blood from tiny blood vessels. Applying a solution of cider vinegar to bruises is a folk remedy that could be worth trying to limit bruising and speed recovery.

Action: Use a cotton pad to apply a solution of 2 tablespoons of cider vinegar in a cup of cool water.

Cancer

Cancer results from mutation of a cell's DNA which allows the cell to continue multiplying instead of dying due to apoptosis (cell suicide) at its allotted time. Such malignant cells arise repeatedly during ordinary everyday life; most are destroyed by the immune system but a few grow into a cancer. Dietary factors that encourage certain cancers include a lack of anti-oxidants such as the flavonoid quercetin, as these normally mop up the free radicals (overactive oxygen particles) that are continually produced in the body and can damage cells.

Several studies suggest that apples have anti-cancer properties and that their antioxidants are partly responsible. Other point to other apple phytochemicals, including pectins, pectin-like rhamnogalacturonans, and triterpenoids. Certainly pectin is broken down by gut bacteria, releasing short-chain fatty acids which raise acidity in the large intestine and thereby encourage apoptosis in colon cancer cells. What's more, experiments indicate that pectins and pectin-like rhamnogalacturonans have pronounced antimutagenic effects.

Many studies have suggested that apples may help prevent cancer, including:

Cancer – general

Finnish research that followed 10,054 people from 1966, found cancer was least likely in those consuming most quercetin. The association between a reduced risk of lung cancer and apple consumption was especially strong.

American Journal of Clinical Nutrition, 2002

Evaluation of the antiproliferative activity of each of 13 apple-peel triterpenoids against liver, breast and colon cancer cells, indicates that each may contribute to the anti-cancer action of whole apples.

Journal of Agricultural and Food Chemistry, 2007

Researchers found that pectin inhibits galactoside-binding lectin 3 ('galectin 3'), a key protein in the progression and spread of cancer in the breast, prostate and colon.

Journal of the Federation of American Societies for Experimental Biology, 2008

Breast cancer

Researchers at Cornell University dosed rats with a breast-cancer inducer (mammary carcinogen) then gave half of them apple extract each day for six months. Tumour incidence was lower in those receiving the apple extract.

Journal of Agricultural and Food Chemistry, 2005

In a recent study at the same university, researchers found that apple extract slowed the growth ('proliferation') of adenocarcinoma breast cancers in rats; such tumours are the main cause of breast-cancer deaths. Consuming the equivalent in humans of one apple a day was associated with non-proliferation of their cancer in 43 per cent of the rats; the equivalent of six apples a day doubled the likelihood of non-proliferation. In contrast, consuming no apple extract was associated with rapid tumour growth in 81 per cent of the rats. Overall, in those rats given apple extract, the tumours were fewer, smaller, slower growing and less malignant.

Journal of Agricultural and Food Chemistry, 2009

Colon cancer

German tests found that adding apple pectin and phenolic compound-rich apple juice to stools encourages production of butyric acid – a short-chain fatty acid that inhibits the cancer-promoter histone.

Nutrition, 2008

Liver cancer

A study at Cornell University found that apples and especially apple peel have potent antioxidant activity and greatly inhibit liver-cancer cell growth.

Journal of Agricultural and Food Chemistry, 2003

Lung cancer

A Hawaiian study of more than 10,000 people found a 40 per cent lower risk of lung cancer in those who ate most apples.

Journal of the National Cancer Institute, 2000

Prostate cancer

Mayo Clinic researchers say quercetin may help prevent or treat prostate cancer growth by blocking androgen hormones.

Carcinogenesis, 2001

A University of Georgia study found that pectin triggered apoptosis ('cell suicide') in up to 40 per cent of prostate cancer cells. It also affected cells that were resistant to hormone therapy, and thus difficult to treat. Researchers are trying to develop a drug that resembles the active part of the most potent type of pectin.

Glycobiology, 2007

Some alternative practitioners believe that diet can influence cancer by changing the body's pH (acid-alkaline) balance. Certainly a cancer itself can be relatively more acidic than normal tissue. But there is currently no scientific evidence to support their view.

Action: Eat an apple a day as this will benefit your general health and it might even help prevent cancer or slow its progression.

Cataract

This clouding of the eye's lens affects many people over 65. Apples might discourage cataracts by helping protect against certain trigger factors, including diabetes, high blood pressure, smoking, infection and sunlight. Their eye-friendly nutrients include vitamins B2 and C, flavonoids and salicylates.

Cider vinegar is an unproven folk remedy for helping to prevent cataracts worsening.

Action: If you would like to try cider vinegar, add it to recipes or take 2 teaspoons in a glass of water 3 times a day for 6 months.

Chronic illness

An apple a day could be wise, because, for example:

A Finnish study that followed 10,054 people from 1966 onwards suggested that eating apples discourages many chronic diseases, including asthma, heart disease, cancer, strokes and diabetes.

American Journal of Clinical Nutrition, 2002

Action: Eat an apple a day as this will benefit your general health and might help prevent certain long-term illnesses.

Cold sores

These lip sores are caused by reactivation of a *Herpes simplex* viral infection by such triggers as stress, periods, infection, skin damage, sunshine and fatigue. Cider vinegar is an old home-remedy for this condition.

Action: Try dabbing neat cider vinegar on your lip 3 times a day with a paper tissue or clean cotton pad if you think a sore is imminent. You could also apply neat cider vinegar to an actual sore, but it might sting.

Colds and sore throat

Chewing an apple makes its pectin swell with water and form a soothing and protective layer of gel on an inflamed throat. This explains its use in certain commercial throat lozenges. An apple's vitamin C might shorten the length of a cold. Another benefit of apples is that fermentation of the pectin in the large intestine releases short-chain fatty acids (such as butyric acid) with 'prebiotic' qualities – meaning they nourish 'good' or 'pro-biotic' bowel bacteria, such as lactobacilli and bifidobacteria. These, in turn, have beneficial effects on the body's immunity.

A German study of 479 volunteers confirmed previous studies in finding that taking probiotic tablets containing lactobacilli and bifidobacteria reduced the severity of colds, shortened their length by two days on average and increased immune cells such as helper T cells.

Clinical Nutrition, 2005

Dr DC Jarvis of Vermont studied 24 people over two years in the 1950s and found their urine pH became highly alkaline before and early on in a cold (*Folk Medicine*). When they followed his suggestion to drink cider vinegar, their urine rapidly returned to its more usual acidic pH and the cold either didn't develop or lasted only a short time. Dr Jarvis attributed this to cider vinegar's organic acids and potassium. A sample of 24 is very small and I can find no other studies to back up this research. But you might in any case like to try taking cider vinegar in the early stages of a cold or sore throat.

A traditional remedy for a sore throat is to gargle with dilute cider vinegar; why this might help is unclear, though cider vinegar does have some antibacterial properties.

Action: Put 1 tablespoon of cider vinegar in a glass of water and sip the mixture over half an hour. Wait half an hour then repeat the treatment. If you dislike cider vinegar in water, add it to soup instead.

Gargle twice a day with a mixture made by putting 1 teaspoon of cider vinegar in a glass of water.

Constipation

An unhealthy diet and dehydration are among the most likely causes. Eating unpeeled raw apples may help, because they are rich in water-soluble types of fibre called pectin and pectin-like compounds. Pectin dissolves in water to form a gel that makes stools softer and easier to pass through and from the bowel. Unpeeled apples also contain cellulose; this insoluble fibre attracts water, which makes stools softer, bulkier and easier to pass, and reduces their 'transit time' through the large intestine.

Cloudy apple juice contains smaller amounts of pectin which may nonetheless be useful.

Action: Include apples and, perhaps, cloudy apple juice in your daily diet.

Corns and calluses

These are usually caused by ill-fitting footwear. Soaking the feet in a solution of cider vinegar is reputed to soften corns and calluses and hasten their demise.

Action: Add a cup of cider vinegar to a large bowl of warm water and soak your feet for 10 minutes a day. Afterwards, rub softened skin from the surface of the corn.

Cough (*see also* Bronchitis and Emphysema)

Vinegar has been used for millennia to fight infections; Hippocrates (460–377 BC), for example, prescribed it for persistent coughs. Apples, too, may help.

Researchers found that a high consumption of fibre and fruit by people with chronic bronchitis was associated with a lesser likelihood of coughing. They believe flavonoids might be partly responsible – and whole apples are rich in flavonoids.

American Journal of Respiratory and Critical Care Medicine, 2004

A five-year study of the eating habits of 63,257 people in Singapore suggested that a diet high in fruit fibre reduces the likelihood of coughs.

American Journal of Respiratory and Critical Care Medicine, 2004

Traditional remedies for a cough involve applying some cider vinegar to the chest or pillow at night. By doing this small amounts of organic acid vapour from the vinegar might be absorbed into the body through the nose or skin, but why this might help remains unclear.

Action: Anyone prone to coughs could try eating 1 or 2 whole unpeeled apples each day.

Another idea – which might seem slightly whacky, but so what if it helps – is to soak some brown wrapping-paper in cider vinegar and put it on your chest. Cover it with a towel, and relax for 20 minutes. Alternatively, try sprinkling a little cider vinegar on to your pillow (covered with an old pillowslip!) each night.

Cramp

Possible triggers include insufficient dietary calcium, magnesium, potassium and vitamins B and C. These are all present in apples, so an apple a day might help.

Cider vinegar is a folk remedy for cramp, possibly because its acidity in the stomach improves calcium and magnesium absorption in the many people who produce sub-optimal levels of their own stomach acid.

Action: Include cider vinegar in recipes or take 2 teaspoons in a glass of water 3 times a day.

You might like to try this folk remedy too: mix 2 tablespoons of vinegar in a cup of warm water, soak a face flannel in this mixture, then put the flannel over the muscle and cover it with a thick towel.

Dandruff

This is often associated with the fungus *Malassezia furfur*. Cider vinegar is a popular home remedy.

Action: Mix 1 cup of cider vinegar with 1 of warm water, apply this solution to the scalp, cover with a towel and wait an hour before rinsing and shampooing. Alternatively, massage neat cider vinegar into the scalp, cover with a towel and leave on for an hour. Repeat once or twice a week.

Diabetes and pre-diabetes

Cider vinegar and apples are proving useful in helping prevent or treat the high blood sugar of pre-diabetes and diabetes. This is important because high blood sugar encourages complications such as disease of the heart, eye and kidney.

A Finnish study of 10,000 people reported a lower risk of diabetes in apple eaters.

American Journal of Clinical Nutrition, 2002

Here are some examples of studies reporting that vinegar lowers blood sugar:

A study of 10 healthy volunteers at Lund University in Sweden found that including vinegar with a white-bread breakfast significantly reduced the expected rises in glucose and insulin afterwards. A vinegar breakfast also slowed absorption of paracetamol. The researchers attributed all this to the vinegar's acetic acid, and recommended eating fermented foods (such as vinegar) to reduce blood sugar and the need for insulin.

European Journal of Clinical Nutrition, 1998

Another study at Lund University found that eating pickled cucumbers with a white bread and yoghurt breakfast dramatically lowered the expected spikes of blood sugar and insulin, while fresh cucumbers had no effect. They concluded this was due to the vinegar in pickled cucumber.

American Society for Clinical Nutrition, 2001

A study at Arizona State University involved 21 people with diabetes or pre-diabetes. Each drank water containing 2 tablespoons of cider vinegar before a carbohydrate breakfast. Vinegar increased insulin sensitivity by 34 per cent in those with insulin resistance and 19 per cent in those with diabetes. They were better able to get sugar from the blood into cells and their blood-sugar and insulin levels improved. Indeed, the blood sugar was 25 per cent lower in those with diabetes, and nearly 50 per cent lower in those with pre-diabetes.

Diabetes Care, 2004

A preliminary study of 12 healthy volunteers at Lund University found that taking vinegar with a white bread breakfast increased satiety; the bigger the dose, the greater the effect.

European Journal of Clinical Nutrition, 2005

A preliminary study at Arizona State University gave 11 people with diabetes 2 tablespoons of cider vinegar and a small piece of cheese before bedtime. Vinegar reduced pre-breakfast blood sugar by 6 per cent next morning, showing its effect is long-lasting.

Journal of the Federation of American Societies for Experimental Biology, 2007

All this suggests vinegar may aid blood-sugar control in people with diabetes, and slow the progression of pre-diabetes to diabetes. One possible explanation is delayed stomach emptying. Another, courtesy of Japanese researchers (*American Society for Nutritional Sciences*, 2000), is that acetic acid inactivates intestinal enzymes (disaccharidases) that convert sugars to glucose. This would help prevent blood sugar rising too high or too quickly, so lowering the need for insulin. Other studies suggest that acetic acid helps normalize the release of sugar from the liver, and the production of sugar in the liver from non-carbohydrate sources.

Other studies show that other acidic foods, including lemon juice, yoghurt, traditionally made slowly fermented bread, and kenkey (fermented corn) also reduce expected blood-sugar spikes after meals; some foods even being as powerful as the oral diabetes drug metformin. Frequent consumption of acidic foods is traditional in many countries and may help explain national differences in diabetes rates. Many such foods contain acetic acid, including Japanese sunomono (vinegar-treated vegetables), sumeshi (vinegared rice), potato salad, mustard, vinegared fish and chips, and vinegar-based dressings.

As for apples, microorganisms in the colon degrade their pectin, liberating short-chain fatty acids such as butyric acid. These help prevent high blood sugar by reducing insulin release and inhibiting the breakdown of stored sugar (glycogen) in the liver. All this helps prevent high blood sugar. Apple juice has less pectin, so raises blood sugar faster. Short-chain fatty acids may help in yet another way, because they inhibit C-reactive protein, a blood marker of inflammation and a predictor of diabetes.

Action: It seems sensible for people with pre-diabetes or dia-betes to eat an apple a day and either add cider vinegar to their food (or drink 2 teaspoons of cider vinegar in a glass of water 3 times a day, with meals), or eat other fermented foods or pickled products containing vinegar.

Diarrhoea

Apple pectin is water-soluble and in the gut it forms a gel that helps bind the bowel contents into stools and thereby reduces bowel-opening frequency. What's more, 'good' bacteria in the gut break down some of the pectin, forming a protective coating for the gut lining which soothes any irritation. This breakdown releases short-chain fatty acids (such as butyric acid) with 'prebiotic' qualities, meaning they nourish 'good' or 'probiotic' bowel bacteria such as lactobacilli and bifidobac-teria. Pectin's prebiotic quality makes colon cells stronger and better able to produce protective mucus which helps prevent irritants sticking to and inflaming the gut lining.

Another type of apple fibre, cellulose, attracts water, bulks up bowel contents and makes them less runny. Cooking apples pre-softens their cellulose, helping it bulk up stools and reduce diarrhoea.

Cider vinegar can help kill diarrhoea-causing bacteria such as *Escherichia coli*, so it's useful for those people (such as one-in-two over-60s) with low production of stomach acid that would otherwise attack bacteria.

Action: If you have diarrhoea, try eating an apple every few hours. Raw apples are good, while cooking the apple first (for example, by stewing or baking it), pre-softens its cellulose, which may be useful if your bowel contents are rushing through very fast.

You might also want to try drinking 2 tablespoons of cider vinegar in a glass of water 3 times a day.

Diverticular disease

In this condition the colon is studded with 'blow-outs' called diverticula. This 'diverticulosis' is usually symptom-free but can make the bowel irritable. The most common complication, diverticulitis, recurs whenever a diverticulum becomes inflamed. Diverticular disease is more likely with increasing age, inactivity and a poor diet that makes the colon unhealthy and encourages constipation.

Apples can be a great help because of their insoluble fibre (such as cellulose) and soluble fibre (such as pectin). Both types help prevent constipation. And the fermentation of pectin by 'good' bacteria in the bowel releases short-chain fatty acids (such as butyric acid) which help nourish and protect colon lining cells.

Action: Eat an apple once or twice a day.

Ear infection

Cider vinegar is a traditional treatment for infection in the outer ear.

Action: Add 2 teaspoons of cider vinegar to an egg cup of water and apply with a cotton bud 3 times a day.

Eczema

Cider vinegar washes are a traditional remedy for eczema. The inflammation of eczema makes the skin's pH (acidity/ alkalinity) rise above its normal slightly acidic pH range of 4.2–5.6. Normal acidity helps prevent infection in eczematous skin by inhibiting the multiplication of potentially harmful bacteria and fungi. Cider vinegar washes have nearly the same pH as normal skin.

Action: Try rinsing the affected area of skin with a mixture of equal volumes of cider vinegar and water twice a day. Avoid broken skin, as this will sting.

Fainting

Simple faints, or the dizziness that warns of them, are often associated with low blood sugar. Eating apples helps prevent this, mainly thanks to their content of the soluble fibre pectin, which helps keep the blood sugar steady by slowing the absorption of sugar from the gut.

Cider vinegar may help too, by slowing the rise in blood sugar after a meal; whether this is due to its acetic acid content or some other constituent is unclear.

Cider vinegar may also help prevent faints in those people – such as one in two over-60s – who have poor digestion caused by low stomach acidity, and who are also 'fast oxidizers' of sugar, meaning they feel hungry sooner after a meal than do most people. This is because its extra acidity improves protein digestion, so they can readily produce energy from protein when they have used up their available sugar.

Action: Eat apples as between-meal snacks, to help maintain normal blood sugar. Include cider vinegar in your main meals.

Fatigue

Apples supply sugar plus small amounts of B vitamins that may help prevent or treat fatigue. More importantly, they supply fibre, which helps keep blood sugar steady, so helping prevent the low-blood-sugar swings sometimes associated with fatigue.

Theoretically, at least, cider vinegar could help tiredness associated with a lack of sufficient stomach acid. This prevents proper absorption of nutrients and is more likely with ageing and stress.

Research at Nagoya University in Japan found that adding acetic acid – the main component of cider vinegar – to the diet of rats enhanced the replenishment of stored sugar (glycogen) in liver and muscle; this suggests cider vinegar might help prevent fatigue associated with endurance exercise.

Journal of Nutrition, 2001

US researchers claim that mineral and vitamin deficiencies acceler-ate age-related decay of mitochondria (the cells' 'power-plants'). Among the most important deficiencies are those of iron, zinc, biotin, pantothenic acid, magnesium and manganese.

Molecular Aspects of Medicine, 2005

London researchers have developed a test (called the ATP profile) to indicate how well mitochondria are working. Their study of 71 people with chronic fatigue syndrome and 53 healthy controls suggested that mitochondrial dysfunction causes chronic fatigue syndrome/myalgic encephalomyelitis.

International Journal of Clinical Experimental Medicine, 2009

Action: See if it helps to eat an apple a day, and to take 2 teaspoons of cider vinegar 3 times a day, as a condiment, in a glass of water, or added to recipes.

Food intolerance

Poor production of stomach acid can occur with stress, prolonged use of antacids or acid suppressants and ageing. Normal levels enable the digestive enzyme pepsin to break down proteins, but a shortage allows poorly digested protein to be absorbed into the blood and trigger allergy.

Action: If you think you might be short of stomach acid, try starting each main meal with a salad sprinkled with a cider vinegar and olive oil dressing, or first drink a glass of water containing 2 teaspoons of cider vinegar. Cider vinegar is considerably less acidic than stomach acid, but can nevertheless aid digestion.

Gallstones

Most gallstones contain cholesterol, others contain bile pigments or calcium salts. The bile often contains excess cholesterol and the gallbladder doesn't contract well. Such problems are more likely with obesity, constipation or diabetes, all of which may be helped by consuming apples and/or cider vinegar as part of a healthy diet.

The apple fibre pectin may bind and thereby help eliminate certain bile acids from the gut, which would prevent them being reabsorbed and used to make gallstones.

A tendency to gallstones may be linked with a lack of stomach acid, because this encourages the gallbladder to be inactive, which in turn encourages the formation of gallstones in the stagnant bile. A lack of stomach acid is more likely with ageing and stress and in people taking antacid or acid-suppressant medication.

Action: Eat an apple a day.

Encourage gallbladder contractions with frequent meals that include something sour (such as cider vinegar) or bitter. If you suspect low levels of stomach acid, take 2 teaspoons of cider vinegar (added to a glass of water or a 'starter') before a meal, to increase stomach acidity. Cider vinegar's pH is 5, whereas stomach acid is more strongly acidic, with a pH of 1–2, but a little extra acid might be useful.

Some people report success from a 'gallbladder flush'. For this, drink 1–2 litres of apple juice a day for 6 days. Next day, miss supper; at 9pm, take 1–2 tablespoons of Epsom salts in a little water; at 10pm, drink 4 fluid ounces of olive oil shaken with 2 of lemon juice, then lie on your left side for 30 minutes before bedtime. This is said to soften stones and let them come out in the stools next day. So far, very few success stories have been verified by x-ray or scan, and 'softened gallstones' in stools may simply be lumps of soap formed from the salts and the oil. Before trying a flush, discuss it with your doctor.

Gum disease

Chewing an apple boosts gum health, because repeated jaw movement increases the circulation of blood to the gums, and apples contain phenolic compounds called tannins which, studies suggest, help prevent periodontal (gum) disease.

Action: An apple a day is good news for your gums!

Hay fever

Cider vinegar is a traditional remedy for allergic rhinitis.

Dr D C Jarvis, of Vermont, studied 24 people over two years in the 1950s and found that their urine pH became highly alkaline before and early on in an allergic attack (*Folk Medicine*). On following his suggestion to drink cider vinegar, their urine rapidly returned to a normal acid pH and the attack was less severe. He attributed this to the organic acids and potassium in cider vinegar.

I can find no confirmatory studies, but it should do no harm for adults to try cider vinegar early in an attack.

Action: Put a tablespoon of cider vinegar into a glass of water and sip the mixture over half an hour. Wait half an hour then repeat. Alternatively, add a tablespoon of cider vinegar to soup or other food.

Headache

Vinegar is a traditional remedy for a headache and familiar from the 'Jack and Jill' nursery rhyme in which Jack mends his head with 'vinegar and brown paper'. Why vinegar should help isn't clear, but some complementary practitioners believe headaches can result from various body 'buffer systems' having to work extra hard to keep the blood's pH (acid-alkaline balance) within its normal tightly controlled range; others believe headaches can result from this pH being at the alkaline end of normal. They recommend various remedies:

Action: Sponge the head with cider vinegar, or apply a flannel soaked in a pint (600ml) of water containing 2 tablespoons of cider vinegar.

Inhale organic-acid vapour by putting a tablespoon of cider vinegar into a vaporizer and staying near for, say, 15 minutes. Or drink a cup of hot water containing 3 teaspoons of cider vinegar 3 times a day.

Head lice

Cider vinegar does not kill lice effectively but can loosen the glue that sticks louse eggs (nits) to hairs.

Action: Add a cup of cider vinegar to a cup of water. Apply to dry hair then leave for half an hour. Wet the hair with water and smooth in lots of silicone-based conditioner (such as Pantene). Comb the hair with a wide-toothed comb, then a fine-toothed one to remove any lice. Now shampoo. Some nits may stay stuck to hairs, so do this wet-combing twice weekly for 2 weeks to catch newly hatched lice.

Heart disease

Coronary heart disease encourages angina and heart attacks. Fatty atheroma collects in coronary artery walls and, when overly thick, the heart muscle no longer gets enough blood to enable it to pump properly. Free radicals in blood oxidize LDL (low-density lipoprotein) cholesterol in atheroma, producing oxidized LDL cholesterol – the dangerous sort. Free radicals are overactive oxygen particles and are encouraged by a poor diet, infection, smoking and stress. They also trigger immune cells to inflame artery walls. Atheroma and inflammation scar and roughen the lining of arteries, which encourages high blood pressure by making arteries less elastic; they also encourage blood clots that can block an artery and cause a heart attack.

Studies suggest that apples and apple juice help protect against heart disease, possibly thanks to their flavonoids such as quercetin and catechins:

Finnish scientists who followed 5,133 initially healthy people for over 20 years found the risk of dying from heart disease was lowest in those who ate the most apples and other flavonoid-rich foods.

British Medical Journal, 1996

A study at UC Davis of 25 healthy people found that when they consumed 12 ounces of apple juice or 2 apples a day, their cholesterol took longer to oxidize. Slow-to-oxidize cholesterol is associated with a reduced risk of heart disease.

Journal of Medicinal Food, 2001

A US survey of nearly 40,000 women for almost 7 years reports that those who consumed apples had a risk of heart disease of up to 22 per cent lower than those who did not eat apples. While this finding was not statistically significant, the researchers thought it warranted further investigation.

American Journal of Clinical Nutrition, 2003

A research review by doctors at Boston University School of Medicine suggests flavonoids improve the behaviour of artery-lining cells and help prevent blood clots. This might help explain any beneficial effects on the cardiovascular disease risk.

American Journal of Clinical Nutrition, 2005

Analysis of 16 years of data on over 34,000 post-menopausal women in the Iowa Health Study, all free from cardiovascular disease at the start, found significant inverse associations between anthocyanidins and coronary heart disease mortality, cardiovascular disease mortality and total mortality; between flavanones and coronary heart disease mortality; and between flavones and total mortality. Apples were among those foods specifically associated with significant reduction in coronary heart disease and cardiovascular disease mortality.

American Journal of Clinical Nutrition, 2007

Another possibility is that aspirin-like salicylates in apple peel may, like aspirin (acetyl salicylic acid), discourage heart attacks associated with inflammation of coronary arteries.

Finally, 'good' microorganisms degrade the apple fibre pectin in the large intestine, freeing useful short-chain fatty acids such as butyric acid. These acids reduce LDL cholesterol (the potentially dangerous sort) and increase HDL cholesterol (the potentially protective sort). They also inhibit C-reactive protein, a blood marker for inflammation and a predictor of cardiovascular disease.

As for cider vinegar:

Researchers at Harvard University who followed up 76,283 women for 10 years found that women who consumed 1 to 2 tablespoons of oil-and-vinegar dressing most days had only half the average risk of heart disease. This salad dressing is a common source of alpha-linolenic acid, a polyunsaturated fat with known heart-health benefits, and the apparent benefit of oil-and-vinegar dressing was attributed to this. But it would be interesting to consider whether the vinegar also played a part.

American Journal of Clinical Nutrition, 1999

Action: You could do your heart a favour by consuming apples and cider vinegar each day.

Heat rash

Vinegar is said to soothe this itchy pimply rash.

Action: Try applying a solution made by adding 1 tablespoon of cider vinegar to a cup of water.

Heavy periods

It's claimed that cider vinegar can ease heavy periods.

Action: If you would like to try this unproven home remedy, drink 2 teaspoons of cider vinegar in a glass of water 2 or 3 times a day, or add cider vinegar to your food.

Hiccups

Possible causes are an overfull stomach, due to eating too much; low stomach acid slowing protein digestion; or fatty, sugary food slowing stomach emptying and encouraging fermentation. Cider vinegar is a traditional remedy.

Action: To try preventing frequent attacks, add cider vinegar to your food, or drink a teaspoon of cider vinegar in a glass of water before a meal. To try stopping hiccups, very slowly sip the same solution or swallow a teaspoon of neat cider vinegar.

High blood pressure

Risk factors include obesity, overactivity of the kidney hormone renin, insulin resistance (pre-diabetes), salt sensitivity, age and genetics, though most often there is no obvious cause. Vinegar can affect several of these factors and preliminary studies suggest it can lower blood pressure.

There are five possible reasons. First, it increases nitric oxide (which relaxes blood vessels). Second, it acts like ACE-inhibitor blood-pressure medication (meaning it inhibits angiotensin-converting enzyme, thereby decreasing production of the blood-vessel constricting hormone angiotensin II). Third, it adds flavour, which helps salt-sensitive people reduce their salt intake. Fourth, adding it to casseroles or stocks containing meat bones releases some of their calcium; this could help the many people who have a low calcium intake, because calcium helps keep blood pressure healthy. Fifth, vinegar could lower blood pressure by encouraging weight loss.

Japanese researchers found that long-term dosage of rats with vinegar or acetic acid lowered blood pressure. They attributed vinegar's effect to its acetic acid. They believe this reduces renin activity, so decreasing angiotensin II. This, in turn, lowers blood pressure by decreasing blood volume and relaxing blood vessels.

Bioscience, Biotechnology, and Biochemistry, 2001

Apples can help lower high blood pressure by contributing potassium (which helps regulate body fluids), magnesium (which relaxes blood vessel walls) and fibre.

Action: If you would like to try cider vinegar, add it to your food 2 or 3 meals a day, or take a teaspoon in a glass of water 3 times a day.

Eat an apple a day.

High cholesterol

Apples can help prevent high cholesterol. People with an unhealthy balance of LDL (low-density lipoprotein) and HDL (high-density lipoprotein) cholesterol, tend to develop a cholesterol-rich layer of atheroma in their arteries. This impairs their circulation. Also, the presence of oxidized LDL cholesterol in atheroma stiffens arteries and encourages high blood pressure, heart attacks and strokes.

Pectin in apples, and to a lesser extent in cloudy apple juice, absorbs cholesterol and triglycerides in the gut and eliminates them from the body. One way it does this is by increasing the viscosity of the contents of the small intestine, which reduces the absorption of cholesterol from food or bile. Another is that 'good' microorganisms degrade pectin in the large intestine, liberating short-chain fatty acids (such as butyric acid) which inhibit cholesterol absorption, suppress cholesterol production in the liver, and boost HDL cholesterol.

Studies using whole apples show that a combination of pectin and vitamin C lowers cholesterol more than does pectin alone; and the combination of pectin and phenols lowers cholesterol and triglycerides more than either alone. The decreases are small but worthwhile. Eating one large apple a day lowers cholesterol by up to 11 per cent. Eating two lowers cholesterol by up to 16 per cent. The cholesterol-lowering effect of four a day can equal that of a statin drug!

In a study at the University of California Davis, volunteers who consumed 2 apples or 12oz of apple juice a day demonstrated significant slowing of cholesterol oxidation. The protective effect reached its peak after 3 hours and dropped off after 24, backing the oft-repeated advice to 'eat an apple a day'.

Journal of Medicinal Food, 2000

Japanese researchers found that giving rats acetic acid (as in vinegar) lowered their cholesterol and triglycerides. Further tests revealed inhibition of production of triglyceride fats (now properly known as triacylglycerols) from sugar in the liver, and an increase of bile in the gut. We don't yet know if vinegar lowers blood pressure in humans, or, if it does, how.

British Journal of Nutrition, 2006

Some alternative practitioners explain that cholesterol is an acidic by-product of fat metabolism. They say a healthy diet containing plenty of alkaline-forming foods (such as apples and cider vinegar) makes the body better able to prevent atheroma accumulating in the arteries, and to dissolve or neutralize and then eliminate cholesterol.

Action: Eat 1 or 2 apples a day.

Indigestion and heartburn

Stewed apple is a favoured first food after a gastrointestinal infection. And organic acids in apples (for example, malic and tartaric) and cider vinegar (acetic acid) may help prevent indigestion caused by low stomach-acid production. Low stomach acid is encouraged by ageing, stress and prolonged use of antacids or acid-suppressant medication. Organic acids such as those in vinegar are weaker than gastric acid, but help provide an acidic environment for efficient protein digestion. Finally, pectin in apples and cloudy apple juice helps keep the gut free from sticky residues which make it sluggish. It also helps prevent potentially harmful bacteria binding to the gut lining.

Heartburn is a frequent symptom of low stomach acid. Medical treatment is to suppress gastric acid with antacids, but this sometimes does no good or even worsens the problem. If antacids don't help, you may have low stomach acid. Consuming vinegar could then help by increasing your stomach acidity, though because its pH is only around 5, it cannot make the stomach as acidic as gastric acid (pH 1–2).

Action: Eat an apple a day.

To use cider vinegar to prevent problems, take 2 teaspoons in a glass of water before each meal, or add it to food.

If you have indigestion or heartburn, take 1 tablespoon in a glass of water. If it helps, the odds are that a lack of stomach acid was to blame.

Irritable bowel syndrome (IBS)

Possible symptoms include pain, constipation, diarrhoea, passing mucus, bowels never feeling empty, wind and bloating. One in three people sometimes have an irritable bowel; one in five of these have frequent trouble – which is then called irritable bowel syndrome (IBS).

Apples' soluble pectin fibre may reduce symptoms, partly because it makes stools softer and easier to pass.

Action: Try eating an apple a day.

Itching

Applying cider vinegar is said to help relieve itching.

Action: Try bathing in tepid bath water containing a cup of cider vinegar.

Or try applying neat cider vinegar to itchy skin, keeping it away from your eyes or other delicate parts.

Kidney stones

Cider vinegar is said to help dissolve common, calcium-containing stones. These are more likely when threatened overacidity of body fluids leads to calcium being withdrawn from bones and teeth and excreted in the urine to keep the body-fluid's pH (acid-alkaline balance) within its normal tightly controlled range. Cider vinegar, unlike other vinegars, is said to have a mild alkalinizing effect after it has been digested, so it might reduce the body's need to take calcium from bones. It might also help by reducing spikes of insulin in the blood after eating carbohydrate. Such foods otherwise raise insulin – a hormone that encourages stones by making the kidneys discharge more calcium in the urine.

Apples and apple juice may help prevent or dissolve stones, as they too have an alkalinizing effect. They also provide vitamin B_6 and magnesium; this might help because, according to researchers, a lack of these nutrients encourages stones.

Action: Try including cider vinegar, apples and apple juice in your diet if you are prone to kidney stones.

Low immunity

Apples may boost immunity. First, their vitamin C is useful for immunity. Second, their pectin fibre is degraded by 'good' microorganisms in the large intestine, liberating short-chain fatty acids such as butyric acid. These aid immunity by stimulating production in the spleen of helper T cells, antibodies, white blood cells and cytokines. They also inhibit C-reactive protein, a blood marker of inflammation

Action: Eat an apple a day.

Memory loss

Anecdotal reports suggest that cider vinegar can aid memory. As for apples and apple juice:

Researchers at the University of Massachusetts suspect that nutrients in apples and apple juice improve memory and learning in mice, and protect against the oxidative damage that contributes to age-related brain disorders such as Alzheimer's. Consuming apple juice protected against oxidative stress and slightly improved memory and learning, possibly by increasing the brain neuro-transmitter (nerve-message carrier) acetylcholine. The amount was comparable to humans drinking two 8oz glasses of apple juice or eating 2 to 3 apples a day

Journal on Nutrition, Health and Aging, 2004

Action: There's only very preliminary evidence that apples, apple juice and cider vinegar can improve memory or slow its loss, but nothing to be lost by including them in your diet.

Metabolic syndrome

This collection of symptoms greatly encourages diabetes, heart disease and strokes. It affects one in five of us overall and is also known as insulin resistance syndrome and syndrome X. It's more likely with increasing age and can be associated with polycystic ovary syndrome. Diagnosis is based on having some combination (subject to debate) of high fasting blood sugar (pre-diabetes), high blood pressure, an apple-shaped body, low HDL-cholesterol and high triglyceride blood fats. Most people who have this syndrome are sedentary, obese and insulin-resistant, though it's unclear whether obesity and insulin resistance are causes or consequences of a more general problem. Some researchers think inflammation and oxidation are involved. Certainly, affected people are more likely to have a raised level in the blood of C-reactive protein, which indicates inflammation.

The US National Health and Nutrition Examination Survey (1999–2004) revealed a 27 per cent decrease in risk of metabolic syndrome among regular consumers of apples, apple sauce and apple juice. They also had a 30 per cent lower likelihood of high diastolic blood pressure; a 36 per cent lower likelihood of high systolic blood pressure; a 21 per cent lower likelihood of a large waist; and lower levels of C-reactive protein, an indicator of inflammation.

Experimental Biology meeting, 2008

Action: It makes sense to eat an apple a day just in case it is protective.

Nosebleed

There are isolated reports that cider vinegar helps stem a nosebleed. Also, consuming cider vinegar is a traditional remedy for frequent nosebleeds

Action: To see if cider vinegar helps stop a nosebleed, soak a cotton-wool ball in cider vinegar, lean your head backwards, then put the cotton-wool ball in the affected nostril.

If you suffer from frequent nosebleeds, try drinking 2 teaspoons of cider vinegar in a glass of water 3 times a day for, say, 3 months.

Osteoporosis

In this condition, affected bone is light and fragile and its cells are destroyed faster than they are created. Risk factors include age, too much or too little exercise, smoking, too little bright outdoor light, a lack of bone-friendly nutrients (calcium, magnesium, zinc, vitamins C, D and K and plant hormones), an early menopause, anorexia and various medications and illnesses (including gut and thyroid disorders). Research increasingly points to inflammation and oxidation being involved.

Apples might help prevent osteoporosis or slow its development because of their antioxidants such as flavonoids, which counter inflammation and oxidation. Apples also contain the trace mineral boron, which researchers believe could improve oestrogen levels and reduce the loss of bone-friendly minerals in the urine. Another constituent, present in small amounts, is the phyto-oestrogen genistein. The rate of loss of bone density around the menopause is much lower in women with a high intake of plant oestrogens; apples contain only small amounts, nevertheless they might help as part of a healthy diet. Apple pectin is useful too, because good gut bacteria break this down, releasing short-chain fatty acids which raise acidity in the large intestine and thereby boost absorption of minerals such as calcium and magnesium.

Cider vinegar might be useful too. First, it renders calcium from food or in supplements more soluble and thus better absorbed. Second, it provides extra acidity in the stomach, which is useful for people in whom a lack of stomach acid causes poor absorption of calcium and certain other nutrients. Third, although vinegar is acidic, the net result of its digestion and metabolism is mildly alkaline.

French researchers report that the phenolic compound phlorizin, found only in apples, prevents bone loss associated with inflammation in rats. If true in humans too, then eating apples might help prevent or treat osteoporosis.

Calcified Tissue International, 2005

Action: It's worth including apples and cider vinegar in your daily diet to help prevent or treat osteoporosis.

Overweight and obesity

Apples contain the soluble fibre, pectin, which slows the absorption of sugar from the gut. This helps prevent hunger and overeating. Pectin can also interfere with the absorption of fat. One theory is that this is because pectins form a gel in the stomach, which mops up triglyceride fats and stops them being absorbed.

Researchers in Texas found that taking pectin increased satiety.

Journal of the American College of Nutrition, 1997

Researchers in Rio de Janeiro reported that overweight middle-aged women on a weight-loss diet who ate 3 apples or pears a day lost more weight.

Nutrition, 2003

Vinegar has been said for thousands of years to promote weight loss. Early research suggests that if cider vinegar does indeed help, it does so by aiding satiety after eating, by helping the body burn calories faster and by helping compensate for any lack of stomach acid.

Low acidity in the stomach affects around one in two over-60s, and is encouraged by stress and prolonged use of antacid or acid-suppressant medication. Research associates low stomach acidity with poor absorption of many nutrients (including protein, vitamins B and C, calcium, iron, magnesium, zinc, copper, chromium, selenium, manganese, vanadium, molybdenum and cobalt). It also indicates that poor nutrient absorption can make people want to eat even when they are not hungry. Cider vinegar improves absorption of these nutrients by increasing stomach acidity. And by improving protein digestion, it may specifically help people who are 'fast oxidizers' of sugar and tend to feel very hungry within three hours or so of a meal. This is because they can readily produce energy from protein when they have used up their available sugar.

Cider vinegar also aids absorption of fats and vitamins A and E by stimulating the release of bile and pancreatic enzymes into the gut. It also slows the rise in blood sugar after a meal. This not only helps prevent high blood sugar, but also the low-blood-sugar swing that sometimes follows, and which can trigger desire to overeat. Whether its blood-sugar-lowering ability is due to its acetic acid or another constituent is unclear.

Japanese research suggests that acetic acid lowers blood sugar by reducing the activity of disaccharidases (enzymes which break complex sugars into simple sugars prior to absorption).

Journal of Nutrition, 2000

When 12 volunteers took 2 tablespoons of vinegar before a carbohydrate-rich meal, they had lower than expected levels of glucose and insulin, and their feeling of fullness more than doubled.

European Journal of Clinical Nutrition, 2005

A study of 18 people at Southern Utah University examined how acids in vinegar, pickle juice, acetic acid, lemon and lime juice, and a placebo, affect the expected blood sugar after a carbohydrate snack. Only vinegar significantly lowered it, which suggests that compounds in vinegar other than acetic acid must contribute to the effect.

Journal of the Federation of American Societies for Experimental Biology, 2006

A report claims that women in their 50s gained 5 pounds less over 10 years if they took more than 500mg of calcium supplements than if they did not. This suggests that people with low stomach acid might lose weight more easily if they improve their calcium absorption by taking vinegar with meals.

On-line report of work at the Fred Hutchinson Cancer Research Center in Seattle, 2006

Japanese researchers report that mice given both a high-fat diet and acetic acid each day for six weeks gained a lot less body fat than did mice given a high-fat diet but no vinegar. They also noted that the acetic-acid group had increased activation ('upregulation' or 'turning on') of genes which produce proteins that break down fats. These findings lead them to believe that acetic acid activates genes that break down fats.

Journal of Agricultural and Food Chemistry, 2009

Action: It's worth including apples and cider vinegar in your diet if you would like to maintain or achieve a healthy weight.

Parkinson's disease

This results from degeneration of brain cells that produce the neurotransmitter (nerve-message carrier) dopamine. There's usually no apparent cause but scientists believe genes and brain infection can play a part.

Studies suggest an apple a day helps reduce the risk of neurodegenerative disorders such as Parkinson's.

A study at Cornell University in the US compared how 2 groups of rat nerve cells fared against hydrogen peroxide, a common oxidator.

One group was pre-treated with apple phenolic extracts; the higher the concentration of the apple extract, the greater the protection against oxidation.

Journal of Food Science, 2004

A study at the same university found the antioxidant quercetin seemed mainly responsible for the above protection, and was better than vitamin C at protecting nerve cells. Apples are rich in quercetin.

Journal of Agricultural and Food Chemistry, 2004

Action: Eat an apple a day.

Peptic ulcer

Thick mucus normally protects the stomach and duodenum from stomach acid and the digestive enzyme pepsin. An ulcer can develop if something interferes with this mucus or with the lining cells or the volume of acid. The usual culprit is inflammation from infection with *Helicobacter pylori* bacteria. This is a major cause of stomach ulcers, stomach inflammation (gastritis) and stomach cancer. Around 2 in 5 of us are infected, though only 1 in 10 infected people develop an ulcer. Some people with ulcers make too much acid, but most don't, and some make too little.

Japanese research shows a strong correlation between low stomach acidity and increased rates of *H. pylori* infection.

Biotechnic and Histochemistry, 2001

It's theoretically possible that if someone with peptic ulcer symptoms tests positive for *H. pylori* and suspects a lack of stomach acid (for example, because acid-suppressants don't relieve symptoms), the acidity of cider vinegar might discourage the infection. But it might temporarily worsen ulcer pain.

Action: If you would like to try it, either drink a glass of water containing 2 teaspoons of cider vinegar each day, or use cider vinegar as a condiment or add it to recipes.

Piles

These painful swollen veins in the lining of the back passage are often associated with constipation.

Action: Including apples in your diet could make all the difference to the problem.

Smelly feet

Cider vinegar soaks are said to reduce foot odour for some hours.

Action: Soak your feet when necessary in a bowl of hot water plus a cup of cider vinegar.

Sprains

Cider vinegar is said to relieve pain from a sprain, though why is unclear.

Action: Apply a cider vinegar compress to the affected area – for example, a face flannel squeezed out in a bowl of hot water plus a cup of cider vinegar.

Stings

Applying cider vinegar is a traditional way of treating a wasp sting. A bee sting requires bicarbonate of soda – baking soda – instead. An easy way to remember is 'V' for 'vasp' stings and vinegar, 'B' for bicarbonate and bee stings. One possible mechanism is that it can convert certain toxins in wasp venom to less toxic acetate compounds.

Dousing with vinegar is a folk remedy for most jellyfish stings as it deactivates venom cells. But immersing the stung part in hot water, if available, for four minutes, is even more effective. Don't put vinegar on a sting from a Portuguese man-of-war jellyfish, though, since researchers say this could make the venom cells that are embedded in the skin discharge more venom.

Action: Apply neat cider vinegar to a wasp or jellyfish sting, using a cotton pad.

Strokes

A stroke ('brain attack') usually results from a blood clot interrupting the blood flow in one of the brain's blood vessels (thrombotic stroke). Less often it is caused by bleeding in the brain from an unhealthy artery (haemorrhagic stroke). The main culprit behind a thrombotic stroke is the narrowing of an artery by atheroma. This fatty substance contains low-density lipoprotein cholesterol, which is readily oxidized by free radicals, making arteries inflamed, scarred and rough inside. Clots form on roughened artery walls, especially if blood is abnormally sticky. Risk factors include smoking, stress, unhealthy diet, obesity, high blood pressure, diabetes and chronic infections.

A Finnish analysis of the diet and health of 9,208 men over a period of 28 years found the lowest risk of thrombotic stroke in those who ate most apples.

European Journal of Clinical Nutrition, 2000

Preliminary evidence suggests that apples and cider vinegar help prevent high blood pressure, obesity and diabetes, so it's worth adding them to your diet.

Action: Include apples and cider vinegar in your daily diet.

Ulcerative colitis

Consuming apples might help ulcerative colitis, thanks to their content of the soluble fibre pectin.

People with mildly to moderately active ulcerative colitis became less reliant on other therapies when they took a supplement of soluble fibre, fish oil and antioxidants.

Clinical Gastroenterology and Hepatology, 2005

Action: Try eating an apple a day.

Varicose veins

Cider vinegar is a traditional remedy for aching varicose veins, though why it might work is not clear.

Action: Dampen a small towel with cider vinegar and wrap it over troublesome veins twice a day, for half an hour each time. Also, either drink a glass of water containing 2 teaspoons of cider vinegar 3 times a day, or use cider vinegar as a condiment or in recipes.

Warts

There are many anecdotal reports of cider vinegar curing warts, but I can find no scientific evidence supporting its use. Some podiatrists use a more corrosive relative of acetic acid, dichloroacetic acid, to treat verrucas and other warts.

Action: Soak some cotton wool in cider vinegar and apply to the wart. Cover with a sticking plaster overnight. Repeat each night for 2 weeks.

CHAPTER THREE

Beauty Aid

Apples and cider vinegar are not only valuable for our health but also have a rightful place in the beauty parlour.

The main reason that cider vinegar is such a popular beauty aid is that its organic acid concentration of about 5 per cent helps maintain the skin's natural acidity. Most other vinegars – except, for example, naturally fermented wine vinegar – are more acidic than this and therefore unsuitable for skin care. Normal skin has a slightly acidic surface layer called the 'acid mantle' or hydro-lipid film. This contains:

- The fatty acids of skin oil (sebum)

- Lactic acid and various amino acids from sweat

- Amino acids and pyrrolidine carboxylic acid from 'cornifying' (hardening) skin cells.

The skin's acid mantle has a pH (acid/alkaline balance) of 4.5–5.75 over most of the body. (A 'neutral pH is 7; below this is acidic, above is alkaline). The pH of the skin in the armpits and around the genitals is around 6.5, which is less acidic. Normal skin pH tends to be slightly more acidic in men than in women.

Normal acidity helps activate the enzymes that enable the production of the lipids (oily fats) present in the skin's hydrolipid film. It also encourages skin to repair itself after mechanical or chemical damage. All this is important, because intact healthy skin is relatively impermeable. This means that water is much less able to escape through the skin (other than via perspiration), and potentially harmful substances and microorganisms are less able to get in. Normal skin acidity also encourages a normal skin flora – the typical populations of various bacteria and fungi that inhabit healthy skin. A normal skin flora helps prevent potentially harmful microorganisms from multiplying and causing infections.

Any loss of normal skin acidity encourages drying, cracking and itching. What's more, eczema or other inflammation tends to make skin more alkaline. Washing with most types of soap increases this alkalinity and makes the skin even more vulnerable to irritation and infection.

Most soaps, even 'mild' soaps, glycerine soaps, 'baby soaps' and 'beauty bars', have an alkaline pH of 7–9. Washing with such soap destroys the skin's protective acid mantle. Healthy, unbroken skin can recover from this increase in pH but the restoration of normal acidity takes time – generally between half an hour and two hours or more; and twice-daily washing with alkaline soap slightly reduces the restored acidity level. Certain soaps are even more alkaline, with a pH of 9.5–11, so they compromise skin acidity even more. The pH of Dove soap is 6.5-7.5, which is relatively low for a bar soap. Only a very few bar soaps (for example, Cetaphil and Aquaderm), have a pH similar to that of normal skin.

However, the pH of many liquid soaps, non-soap cleansers and bath and shower gels is closer to that of normal skin; and a few, for example, Johnsons pH 5.5 Hand Wash, have a pH similar to that of normal skin. Using a home-made skin cleanser containing cider vinegar avoids the loss of normal acidity that accompanies washing with most types of soap. Another idea, if you want to continue using alkaline soap, is to rinse your skin afterwards with a home-made skin splash containing cider vinegar, so as to restore the skin's normal acidity.

Cider vinegar can also restore acidity to hair that has been washed with an alkaline shampoo. Most shampoos are alkaline and can leave newly washed hair dull and lacklustre. They also temporarily destroy the normal acidity of the scalp, leaving it more prone to dryness, irritation and infection. However, a cider vinegar rinse can make the hair shinier than it would otherwise be. It can also enhance natural highlights in hair.

Because of its antibacterial properties, cider vinegar also has deodorizing properties that are particularly useful for armpits and feet.

Skin cleansing

- Make a cleansing rub for soiled hands by moistening half a cup of oatmeal with cider vinegar. Use a larger quantity of oatmeal if you want to cleanse your whole body this way.

- Put a cup of cider vinegar in the bath water, immerse a flannel (wash-cloth) in the water and use it to cleanse your skin.

Skin rinsing

- Wash in a shower or unplugged bath and rinse yourself with water. Then fill the bath with water, add half a cup of cider vinegar, lie in the bath and relax.

- Alternatively, wash in the bath or shower. Then rinse yourself with warm water and half a cup of cider vinegar poured from a large plastic jug.

Skin toning

- If you usually use cleansing cream or lotion on your face, follow this by applying a skin toner made by adding 4 tablespoons of cider vinegar to half a pint (250ml) of cold water. Keep the skin toner in a capped glass or plastic bottle, and apply it with a soft cotton cloth or cotton wool.

- Alternatively, use a scented toner. Make the toner as above, put it in a saucepan and add half a tablespoon of dried rosemary leaves or lavender flowers, or 1 tablespoon of fresh leaves or flowers. Bring to the boil and simmer for 5 minutes, then cool and bottle.

Hair rinsing

- After shampooing, rinse your hair with a 1 pint (500ml) jug of warm water to which you have added 2 tablespoons of cider vinegar.

Deodorizing

- Wash your armpits, and then apply either neat cider vinegar, or cider vinegar in which you have steeped some rosemary or mint leaves, or lavender flowers, for 2 weeks.

- Wash your feet, then soak them for 5–10 minutes in a basin of water containing half a cup of cider vinegar.

CHAPTER FOUR

Household Help

Cider vinegar can make certain household chores easier and save the expense of buying household maintenance products.

Air-freshening

- Half fill a spray bottle with water and add a teaspoon of baking soda (sodium bicarbonate) and a tablespoon of cider vinegar. Shake the open bottle to mix the contents. When the foaming stops, fill the bottle with water and put on the cap. Use as an air freshener to help eliminate the smell of smoke, pets, cooking and other unwanted odours.

- Make a fragrant freshener by adding to a saucepan 2 pints of water, 2 tablespoons of cider vinegar and 50g (2oz) fresh, or 25g (1oz) dried, lavender, thyme, rosemary or cloves. Bring to the boil and simmer for 10 minutes. Cool, strain, put into a spray bottle and use as desired.

- Rid your hands of the smell of onions, garlic or fish by pouring cider vinegar into your cupped hand, rubbing them together, and washing with soapy water.

- Add a splash of cider vinegar to soapy water then use this to wipe kitchen worktops or other hard surfaces to rid them of food smells or other unwanted odours.

- When painting a room, reduce paint odour by standing a bowl of cider vinegar somewhere safe.

Cleaning

- Rub soiled collars and cuffs with a paste of equal parts of cider vinegar and baking soda (sodium bicarbonate). Wait for 30 minutes then wash as normal.

- Reduce perspiration stains on clothing by soaking garments for several hours in a basin of water containing half a cup of cider vinegar.

- Freshen and clean floors by adding a cup of cider vinegar to the cleaning water.

- Help to keep sink and basin drains clear by pouring half a cup of baking soda (sodium bicarbonate) down the plughole, then half a cup of hot cider vinegar (heated for a minute in the microwave). Leave for half an hour and then flush with a kettle of just-boiled water.

- Add half a cup of cider vinegar to dish-washing water to cut grease and reduce the amount of washing-up liquid needed.

Disinfecting

- Immerse a smelly flannel, sponge or dishcloth in half and half of cider vinegar and water. Leave for two hours and then rinse with water.

- Help prevent mould discolouring bathroom tile grout by spraying tiles twice a week with water containing two tablespoons of cider vinegar.

- Clean a mildewed shower curtain by putting it in the washing machine along with a large bath towel. Before you start, add 4oz (100g) bicarbonate of soda to the washing powder in the dispenser. Then wash the load on a low-temperature setting, adding 100ml cider vinegar to the fabric-softener dispenser during the rinse cycle.

Dishwasher care

- Clean a smelly dishwasher or its dispenser with a brush and soapy water, then add a cup of cider vinegar to the empty machine and run a cycle to remove odours.

Cleaning semi-permanent plaits, or dreadlocks

- Fill a spray bottle with 1 part cider vinegar and 4 parts water. Spray plaits or dreadlocks generously, leave for 10 minutes, then rinse well. This helps remove grease and hair products such as wax.

Fabric softening

- Mix 2 tablespoons of cider vinegar, 2 tablespoons of baking powder (bicarbonate of soda) and 4 tablespoons of water. Add to the final rinse water if washing by hand, or to the fabric-softener dispenser of a washing machine, to leave fabrics soft and static-free.

Glass cleaning

- Wipe window glass, spectacle lenses, or mirrors with a mixture of 1 part cider vinegar to 3 parts water, then dry with newspaper or a slightly damp towel.

Insect repelling

- Repel fleas by adding half a cup of cider vinegar to the final rinsing water when shampooing your dog.

Limescale removing

- Soften limescale around taps by covering overnight with a paper towel soaked in cider vinegar; next morning the limescale should be much easier to remove.

- Help clear limescale from a steam-iron's reservoir by filling it with cider vinegar. Turn on the iron, let it steam until dry, then rinse the reservoir with clean water.

Polishing

- Shine up wooden furniture by adding a few drops of cider vinegar to commercial polish.

- Polish wooden furniture with half and half cider vinegar and paraffin.

- Brighten copper and brass by applying a paste made of equal parts of salt, flour and cider vinegar. Let the paste dry for 10 minutes, then buff with a polishing cloth.

Rust removing

- Help remove rust by immersing small metal objects in cider vinegar for several hours.

Colour setting

- When washing coloured fabric add a cup of cider vinegar to help set the dye so it won't leach out and stain other fabrics.

Stain removing

- Wipe salt-stained shoes with a cup of water containing a tablespoon of cider vinegar.

- Clean stained stainless-steel, or copper-coated pans and bowls with a paste of salt and cider vinegar.

- Try removing ink, grass, coffee, tea, fruit and berry stains from fabric by soaking the stain in cider vinegar for an hour, then washing.

- Clean brown stains inside a tea or coffee pot by filling it with half and half cider vinegar and water. Leave for half an hour then rinse.

Sticky-stuff remover

- Loosen stickers or remnants of their glue by gently scrubbing with cider vinegar.

- Use cider vinegar to remove the resin and hardener components of two-part epoxy glue, or even not-yet-set glue. (If any of these touch your eye or skin, irrigate the area immediately and generously with water).

- Loosen chewing gum or its stains on clothes by rubbing with cider vinegar before laundering.

Tights

- Make tights longer-lasting and less ladder-prone by adding a tablespoon of cider vinegar to the final rinse water when washing.

Washing machine care

- If your washing machine or its dispenser is smelly, clean with a brush and soapy water, then add a cup of cider vinegar to the empty machine and run a cycle to remove the odour.

- If your washing-machine dispenser is furred up with lime-scale, clean with a brush and soapy water, then add a cup of cider vinegar to the dispenser and run a cycle to help remove the deposits.

Weedkilling

- Kill weeds by spraying with cider vinegar.

Windscreen anti-icer

- Mix 3 parts cider vinegar with 1 part water and use this to wipe over your windscreen.

CHAPTER FIVE

Recipes

From my lifelong interest in cooking, food and nutrition I know that apples, apple juice, cider and cider vinegar are not only very enjoyable but can also improve our health and wellbeing. These tried and tested recipes are worth a place on anyone's table.

Apples

Apples are brilliant on their own and a good complement to many other foods. Crisp dessert apples partner well with cheese, for example, and I suggest you experiment to see which varieties of apple you prefer with which types of cheese. You might start by trying a bronzy russet apple with a chunk of cheddar or nutty wensleydale, a sweet Red Delicious with a piece of Stilton or Dolcelatte, or a tart Granny Smith with some crumbly goat's cheese.

Apples are excellent in fruit salad and you can also add sliced, diced or shredded apple to vegetable salads – such as white, red or green cabbage salad, potato salad, beetroot salad, nut and celery salad and celeriac salad. Apple slices slowly dried in the oven, cooled, then stored in an airtight tin, are a great addition to picnics and lunchboxes. Apples can add a fragrant note to soup, and also form the base of many delicious sorts of chutney, including the apple and ginger chutney below.

Apple sauce is traditional with roast pork, as are roasted whole apples with roast goose, and quartered pan-fried apples with pork chops. But apple sauce is also good with other meats, both hot and cold.

Sweetened stewed apple also makes a quick and easy dessert that's particularly good with custard, cream, or ice cream, or as a filling for pancakes. Apple tarts and pies are always popular and the recipe below for apple and marzipan tart is ideal if you are celebrating.

- Where a recipe says 'dessert' apples, it means any apples that you could enjoy eating on their own.

- Where a recipe says 'cooking' apples, it means apples that are too tart to eat on their own.

SPICED APPLE AND BUTTERNUT SOUP

Apples lend an uncommon sweetness to this unusual and colourful soup. You can have it hot or cold. If you prefer, use 1 tablespoon (15ml) of curry powder instead of the four different spices.

  2oz (50g, (¼ cup) butter
  2 tablespoons olive oil
  1 teaspoon ground cumin
  1 teaspoon ground coriander
  ½ teaspoon ground turmeric
  ½ teaspoon ground fenugreek
  Pinch of black pepper
  1 onion, peeled and sliced
  2 cloves garlic, peeled
  16oz (450g, 2 cups) butternut squash, peeled, deseeded and cut
      into chunks
  3 dessert apples, peeled, cored and sliced
  40fl oz (1.1l, 5 cups) chicken stock (ideally home-made by boiling a
      cooked chicken carcass in water with vegetables and herbs)
  ½ teaspoon dried mixed herbs
  1 tablespoon fresh parsley, chopped, or 4 teaspoons croutons
  6fl oz (180ml, ¾ cup) sour cream – optional

Put the butter and olive oil in a large saucepan and heat until the butter has melted. Add the cumin, coriander, turmeric, fenugreek and black pepper and fry gently for 1 minute. Add the onions and garlic and continue cooking for 10 minutes or until the onions are soft but not brown. Add the butternut squash, apples and chicken stock. Bring to the boil and simmer for 45 minutes. Cool and blend until smooth. Stir in the sour cream and serve hot or cold. Garnish with parsley or croutons.

SWEET AND SOUR RED CABBAGE WITH APPLES

This sweet-and-sour dish from central Europe complements fatty meats such as roast pork, goose and duck. It's a good idea to make double the amount, as it freezes so well.

2oz (50g, ¼ cup) butter
1 large onion, finely sliced
Pinch of ground cloves
Pinch of black pepper
½ teaspoon salt
1 large red cabbage, finely shredded
2 dessert apples, peeled, cored and diced
4oz (100g, ½ cup) brown sugar
7fl oz (210ml, well over ¾ cup) cider vinegar
Water

Melt the butter in a large saucepan. Add the onions, ground cloves, black pepper and salt. Fry gently, stirring occasionally, for 10 minutes, until the onions are soft but not brown. Stir in the cabbage, apples, sugar, cider vinegar, and enough water just to cover the cabbage. Bring to the boil, cover and simmer, stirring occasionally, for 35 minutes. Remove the lid and continue to simmer for a further 10 minutes.

BAKED APPLES

This homely dessert is simple to prepare, fragrant and always welcome. You can ring the changes by stuffing each apple with blackcurrant or blackberry jam plus two teaspoonfuls of lemon juice.

> 4 cooking apples, cored
> 3oz (75g, ½ cup) sultanas or chopped dates
> 2oz (50g, ⅓ cup) walnuts, chopped
> 4oz (100g, just over ½ cup) muscovado sugar
> 1oz (30g, 2 tablespoons) butter, melted
> 5fl oz (150ml, just over ½ cup) cider or water

Pre-heat the oven to 170°C (325°F) Gas Mark 3.

Using a sharp pointed knife, score the skin just above the widest part of each cored apple. Stand the apples in a buttered baking tray and well apart from each other.

Mix the sultanas or dates, walnuts, sugar and butter in a bowl. Use this mixture to fill the cored-out centre of each apple, and pile a little extra on top. Pour the cider or water into the baking tray.

Cook the apples for 30 minutes and serve with vanilla ice cream plus the scraped-out syrupy juices from the baking tray.

APPLE AND MARZIPAN TART

This luxurious treat is perfect for high days and holidays, and if you buy ready-made pastry and marzipan it's easy to prepare.

    1lb (450g) frozen puff pastry, thawed
    8oz (225g) marzipan
    4 red dessert apples
    8oz (225g) apricot jam

Pre-heat the oven to 180°C (350°F, Gas Mark 4).

Roll the pastry into a rectangle just smaller than a non-stick baking tray. Trim the pastry, and reserve the trimmings. Put the pastry on to the baking tray and prick it with a fork. Use a pointed knife to make a cut that is 1 inch (2.5cm) in from around the outside of the pastry.

Using a rolling pin, roll out the marzipan to make a rectangular sheet the same size as the large inner rectangle of pastry. Place the marzipan sheet on the pastry.

Gently heat the apricot jam in a small saucepan until just melted.

Core and thinly slice the unpeeled apples. Lay the slices in overlapping rows on the large inner rectangle of pastry. Cut leaves, hearts or initials from the pastry trimmings, then use these as a decoration over the apples. Using a pastry brush, brush the apricot jam over the apple slices, pastry decorations and pastry rim.

Cook in the oven for 20–25 minutes. Serve warm or cold, with cream.

APPLE CRUMBLE

A good crumble with a crunchy top and soft moist inner layer of sweetened fruit is just the ticket.

> 1lb (450g) cooking apples
> Juice of 1 lemon
> 4oz (100g, 1 cup) muscovado sugar
> 7oz (200g, just under 2 cups) plain flour
> 1 teaspoon baking powder
> 1oz (30g, ¼ cup) ground almonds
> 3oz (75g, just over ¼ cup) butter
> 2oz (50g, ½ cup) oats

Pre-heat the oven to 180°C (350°F, Gas Mark 4).

Peel, core and slice the apples and put them into a buttered ovenproof dish. Stir in both the lemon juice and 1 tablespoon of sugar.

Put the flour, baking powder and ground almonds into a large bowl. Cut the butter into little pieces and rub into the flour and almonds until the mixture resembles fine bread-crumbs. Mix in the remaining sugar, plus the oats.

Level the surface of the fruit mixture and sprinkle the crumble evenly over it.

Bake for about 30 minutes or until the crumble looks golden-brown. Serve with either vanilla ice-cream, custard, or plain yoghurt.

APPLE AND GINGER CHUTNEY

The warmth of the ginger makes eating this chutney with cold meat or cheese a very special treat.

  4lb (1.8kg) cooking apples, peeled, cored and chopped
  20fl oz (600ml, 2½ cups) cider vinegar
  3–4 cloves garlic, peeled and crushed or finely chopped
  1½lb (675g, 3¾ cups) soft brown sugar
  2 teaspoons dried ginger
  ½ teaspoon mixed spice
  Pinch Cayenne pepper

Sterilize glass preserving jars, or jam jars with screw lids, by scalding with just-boiled water.

Put the apples, half the cider vinegar and the garlic into a large saucepan, bring to the boil and simmer for 20 minutes or until thickened. Add the rest of the cider vinegar, and the sugar, ginger, mixed spice and Cayenne pepper and cook for a further 20 minutes.

Put the chutney in the jars and cover with waxed paper discs. When slightly cooled, cover the jars tightly with lids.

APPLE JELLY

Apple jelly is easy to make from tart apples because they are so rich in pectin. Use Bramleys, other tart cooking apples, or crab apples. Eat apple jelly with bread and butter, cheese or cold meat, or add it to the saucepan when making jam from low-pectin fruits such as strawberries, raspberries, apricots, blueberries or cherries. Crab apple jelly is a traditional accompaniment for roast lamb.

4lb (1.8kg) cooking or crab apples, unpeeled, washed, cut into
   chunks
Cold water to cover
1lb (450g, 2 cups) sugar for each 1 pint (600ml, 2½ cups)
   strained juice
Juice of 1 lemon

Sterilize glass preserving jars, or jam jars with screw lids, by scalding with just-boiled water.

Put the apple chunks into a large pan and cover with cold water. Bring to the boil and simmer for 25 minutes, or until the apples are very soft and the liquid is reduced by about a third.

Put the apple pulp into a jelly bag, or a large sieve lined with two layers of muslin, and collect the strained liquid in a pan underneath. Leave to drip overnight. Don't push the apple through to speed collection as this would make the jelly cloudy.

Next day, measure the liquid and put it into a large saucepan. Add the right amount of sugar, plus the lemon juice.

Heat gently, stirring, until the sugar has dissolved. Boil rapidly for 35–40 minutes or until setting point is reached. Test for this by chilling a teaspoon in the fridge, then dipping it quickly into the jelly. Jelly at setting point will set on the back of the spoon.

Remove the froth.

Put the jelly in the jars and cover with wax-paper discs. When slightly cooled, cover the jars tightly with lids.

APPLE JUICE

Add this ambrosial juice to fresh fruit salads, blend it with kiwis, mixed berries, pineapple or other fruits to make juice drinks, and delight in the character it lends to gravy or to stews of beef or pork. Apple juice mixed with a little lemon juice and chopped apple and set with gelatine makes a wonderful jelly. You can also use the juice to make syrups, sauces, mousses, sorbets and ice cream.

APPLE JUICE GRAVY

This is particularly good with pork chops or roast pork.

    300ml (10fl oz, 1¼ cups) apple juice
    2 teaspoons Dijon mustard
    Black pepper
    ¼ teaspoon cinnamon – optional

Remove the meat from the roasting pan or frying pan and keep warm. Put the pan on the hob and add the apple juice, mustard, black pepper, and cinnamon if desired. Bring to the boil and simmer for 10 minutes, or until thickened.

MULLED APPLE JUICE

Heating and spicing transforms apple juice from a drink for the gods to a drink for partying gods.

    2 pints (1.1l, 5 cups) unfiltered apple juice
    2 apples, unpeeled and thinly sliced
    2 oranges, unpeeled and thinly sliced
    2 teaspoons mixed spice
    2 bay leaves
    1 teaspoon vanilla essence
    Cinnamon stick
    2 fl oz (60ml, ¼ cup) dark rum, brandy or apple brandy (optional)
    Few extra orange or apple slices (optional)

Pour the apple juice into a large stainless-steel pan. Add the apples, oranges, mixed spice and bay leaves. Bring to the boil and simmer for 30 minutes, adding the cinnamon stick 5 minutes before the end. Add the vanilla essence. Strain into a cup and add a splash of rum or brandy, if desired. Add the rum or brandy and extra orange or apple slices if desired.

Cider

Cider isn't just a delicious beverage – it's great to cook with too. Substituting it for stock or water adds a fragrant and unusual note to casseroled meat, poultry or vegetables.

Simmer cider in a saucepan until its volume has greatly reduced, then drizzle the resulting intensely flavoured liquid over plain yoghurt, or sweeten it as in the recipe for cider glaze, below. Cider makes a surprisingly attractive sorbet. And good mulled cider is the equal any day of good mulled wine.

CIDER GLAZE

Brush this glaze over boiled ham before roasting, over fish before baking, over cooked fish, over carrots or butternut squash before baking them, or over cooked carrots or squash. It is also good made without honey.

  16fl oz (480ml, 2 cups) cider
  3oz (75g, 1/3 cup) butter
  1 tablespoon clear honey

Pour the cider into a pan and bring to the boil. Simmer until the cider has reduced to about two tablespoons. Remove the pan from the heat, add the honey and butter, and stir until the butter has melted.

GARLICKY CHICKEN CASSEROLE WITH CIDER AND CIDER VINEGAR

Ten cloves of garlic appear to be a lot but they are a vital part of this dish. The cider and cider vinegar contribute different notes to the symphony of flavours.

1oz (25g, 2 tablespoons) butter
2 tablespoons olive oil
2 onions, peeled and sliced
1 stick celery, thinly sliced
2 carrots, peeled and sliced
8 chicken thighs
½ teaspoon black pepper
1½ teaspoons dried tarragon, or 3 teaspoons fresh
10 garlic cloves, peeled
8oz (225g, 2½ cups) mushrooms, sliced
4oz (100g, ⅔ cup) red lentils
20fl oz (600ml, 2½ cups) cider
6fl oz (180ml, ¾ cup) cider vinegar
Water
Small handful fresh parsley, chopped

Pre-heat the oven to 180°C (350°F, Gas Mark 4).

Put the butter and olive oil into an ovenproof casserole and heat until the butter has melted. Add the onions, celery and carrots and cook, stirring occasionally, for 10 minutes. Add the chicken pieces and black pepper and brown the chicken all over. Add the bay leaf, tarragon, garlic, mushrooms, lentils, cider, cider vinegar and enough water just to cover the chicken. Cover the pan and cook in the oven for 1¼ hours.

Garnish with chopped parsley before serving.

CIDER SORBET

Enjoy this refreshing sorbet on its own or with ice cream and a medley of fresh fruit.

  14fl oz (420ml, 1¾ cups) cider
  2oz (50g, just over ¼ cup) light brown sugar
  3 cloves
  2 allspice berries
  1 cardamom pod, crushed
  1 cinnamon stick
  3 teaspoons lemon juice

Bring the cider, sugar, cloves, allspice, cardamom and cinnamon to the boil and simmer for 5 minutes. Cool to room temperature, sieve, and discard the spices. Stir in the lemon juice. Chill and freeze.

MULLED CIDER

This warming drink is a favourite in the US and the UK.

40fl oz (1.1l, 5 cups) cider
Juice of 1 lemon
2oz (50g, just over ¼ cup) brown sugar
1 teaspoon mixed spice
4 cloves
1 cinnamon stick
1½ inch piece of ginger root
Pinch of freshly grated nutmeg

Put the ingredients into a pan, bring to the boil and simmer for 15 minutes. Sieve and discard the cloves, cinnamon stick and ginger root.

Pour into glasses and sprinkle with the nutmeg.

Cider Vinegar

You can use this fragrant tawny vinegar whenever a recipe specifies malt, wine or other vinegar. It's good, for example, for making salad dressings and many sauces – including mayonnaise, mint sauce, mustard and the South American chimichurri.

Sprinkle cider vinegar over fried fish and chips, or over soft herring roes that have been coated with flour then fried in butter and olive oil. And make gravy by adding a couple of tablespoons to the juices in the roasting pan in which you have cooked a joint of lamb.

Cider vinegar is a natural for pickling or marinating various vegetables and fruits. And it's an essential ingredient of many a savoury casserole.

SALAD DRESSING

This dressing makes lettuce leaves, other raw vegetables and other salad ingredients unusually enticing. You can vary it by adding herbs or spices.

6fl oz (180ml, ¾ cup) olive, walnut or corn oil (or a mixture of
    any two)
2 tablespoons cider vinegar
2 teaspoons Dijon mustard
1 teaspoon clear honey
Black pepper

Put the ingredients in a bowl and whisk well with a fork.

BLENDER MAYONNAISE

This home-made mayo is a real treat and is easily made in an electric goblet blender. If you find the flavour of olive oil too strong, use corn or sunflower oil instead.

   2 tablespoons cider vinegar
   1 egg
   2 teaspoons Dijon mustard
   1 teaspoon clear honey
   Black pepper
   6fl oz (180ml, ¾ cup) olive oil, or half and half olive and walnut oils
   2 tablespoons just-boiled water (optional)

Put the cider vinegar, egg, mustard, honey and black pepper in the blender, and blend at high speed for a few seconds until smooth. Continue blending at a lower speed and very slowly pour in the olive oil (or olive and walnut oils).

BONE STOCK

This stock, made with a cooked chicken carcass, or with ham, pork, beef, lamb or fish bones, is very rich in calcium, due to cider vinegar releasing calcium from the bones. Use it as the basis of soup, or add it to casseroles or any other recipes that require stock.

Cooked stripped chicken carcass, other meat bones, or fish bones
2 carrots, peeled and finely sliced
2 onions, peeled and chopped
2 cloves garlic, peeled and crushed or chopped
6fl oz (180ml, ¾ cup) cider vinegar
1 teaspoon dried mixed herbs
Black pepper
½ teaspoon salt

Put all the ingredients into a large saucepan and cover with water. Bring to the boil, cover and simmer for one hour, adding more water if necessary. Strain the stock into a bowl and use at once, or cool and freeze for another time.

CHIMICHURRI

This popular South American barbecue sauce is arguably more of a salsa than a sauce and it's just as delicious made with cider vinegar as with the red wine vinegar that's more often used in countries such as Argentina. Chimichurri can accompany any grilled, roast or barbecued meat or poultry, or you can use it as a pre-cooking marinade. It also makes a flavoursome addition to roast sweetcorn, steamed asparagus or boiled potatoes.

8fl oz (240ml, 1 cup) cider vinegar
8fl oz (240ml, 1 cup) olive oil
½ teaspoon Cayenne pepper
½ teaspoon ground cumin
4 garlic cloves, crushed or finely chopped
1 teaspoon black pepper
1 teaspoon dried oregano or 2 teaspoons chopped fresh oregano
2 tablespoons parsley, finely chopped
1 small onion, finely chopped
1 tomato, chopped

Put the ingredients into a screw-top jar, cover and shake well. Refrigerate for two hours before using.

POTATO SALAD

Make a feast from a bowl of freshly cooked floury potatoes by adding an onion, dill and parsley salsa. This salad is particularly popular in Russia and Germany and good when hot, warm or cold.

6 medium potatoes, peeled
2 onions, peeled and chopped
3 tablespoons fresh dill, snipped up with scissors
3 tablespoons fresh parsley, chopped
Pinch of black pepper
3 tablespoons walnut or olive oil, or half and half
3 tablespoons cider vinegar
1 teaspoon sugar

Put the potatoes in a saucepan of water, bring to the boil and simmer for about 20 minutes, or until soft but not falling apart. Drain the potatoes, cut into thick slices and put into a bowl. Add the onions, dill, parsley and black pepper. Put the olive oil, cider vinegar and sugar into a saucepan and bring to the boil. Pour this mixture over the potatoes.

FONDANT COURGETTES

The basis of this recipe was kindly given to me by the owner of the amazing Blairs Cove House restaurant in Durrus, County Cork, Ireland, after I'd waxed lyrical about it during an evening there. I've adapted the recipe to use cider vinegar instead of malt vinegar, and I promise it's worth every last one of the four days it takes to make. Use to accompany cold meats, herring or cheese.

   6 courgettes, or 1 medium marrow, peeled, deseeded and cut into
      chunks
   2 large onions, peeled and sliced into rings
   3 tablespoons salt
   16fl oz (480ml, 2 cups) cider vinegar
   20fl oz (600ml, 2½ cups) water
   18oz (500g, 2½ cups) sugar
   1 tablespoon curry powder
   1 teaspoon black peppercorns

Sterilize glass preserving jars, or jam jars with screw-on lids, by scalding with just-boiled water.

Day 1
Put the courgettes and onions into a bowl and stir in the salt.

Day 2
Drain in a large colander and rinse well under cold running water. Put the cider vinegar, water, 14oz (400g) sugar, curry powder and black peppercorns into a large saucepan. Bring to the boil, add the courgettes and simmer for 5 minutes. Transfer to a large bowl and cool at room temperature.

Day 3
Stir 4oz (100g) sugar into the mixture in the bowl.

Day 4
Put the mixture into a large saucepan, bring to the boil, and boil for 5 minutes. Put the mixture into the jars. Cool slightly and cover tightly with lids.

APRICOT RELISH

A spoonful of apricot relish makes a wonderful addition to roast lamb or pork, or potatoes roasted in their skins with garlic and thyme. It is equally good served hot or cold.

5oz (150g, 1 cup) dried apricots
6fl oz (180ml, ¾ cup) apple juice
6fl oz (180ml) cider vinegar
2oz (50g) soft brown sugar
1 teaspoon dried cinnamon
1 teaspoon freshly grated nutmeg
Pinch of black pepper
½oz (12.5g) butter

Put the apricots, apple juice, cider vinegar and sugar in a saucepan. Bring to the boil and simmer gently for 10 minutes. Cool a little. Put into a blender, add the cinnamon, nutmeg and butter and whizz until smooth. If you prefer to serve the relish hot, return it to the pan and heat gently.

CUCUMBER PICKLE

This is brilliant with cold savoury food and a sure-fire hit whether served for solo repasts, family meals or festive gatherings.

2lb (900g) cucumber, peeled and finely sliced

2lb (450g, 3 cups) onions, finely sliced

2 tablespoons salt

15fl oz (450ml, just under 2 cups) cider vinegar

12oz (350g, 3½ cups) brown sugar

½ teaspoon ground turmeric

½ teaspoon ground cloves

4 teaspoons mustard seed

4 teaspoons celery seed (optional, but worthwhile if you can get it)

Sterilize glass preserving jars, or jam jars with screw-on lids, by scalding with just-boiled water.

Put the cucumber, onions and salt into a bowl, mix well and leave for 3 hours. Rinse well in cold running water and drain in a sieve.

Put the cucumber and onions into a large saucepan, add the cider vinegar and bring to the boil. Simmer gently for 20 minutes. Add the sugar, turmeric, cloves, mustard seed and celery seed and stir until the sugar has dissolved. Bring to the boil then simmer for 2 minutes.

Remove the cucumber and onions with a slotted spoon and put into the warm glass jars. Simmer the remaining syrup for 15 minutes, then pour it over the cucumber and onions. Cover the jars tightly.

BEETROOT AND HORSERADISH RELISH (CWIKLA OR RED CHRAIN)

This colourful accompaniment for fish, meat or cheese originated in eastern Europe and in Russia. Once you've tried it the odds are high you'll be a big fan.

1lb (500g) raw beetroot
2 tablespoons horseradish sauce
1 tablespoon wholegrain mustard
2fl oz (60ml, ¼ cup) cider vinegar
1 tablespoon sugar
Plenty of black pepper

Boil the beetroots in their skins for 30 minutes or until tender when tested with a knife. Leave to cool, then rub off the skins and grate the beetroot.

Stir the horseradish sauce, mustard, cider vinegar, sugar and pepper into the grated beetroot.

MARINATED PEARS

Tickle your taste buds by eating these sweet-and-sour pears with cold meat, sausage or cheese.

  2lb (1kg) hard pears, peeled, cored and quartered
  Water to cover
  Sugar
  1 pint (550ml, 2½ cups) cider vinegar
  1 pint (550ml, 2½ cups) water
  1lb (450g, 2¼ cups) sugar
  1 clove
  Pinch of cinnamon
  Bay leaf
  1 teaspoon peppercorns
  Pinch of salt

Sterilize glass preserving jars, or jam jars with screw-on lids, by scalding with just-boiled water.

Cover the pears with water in a pan, bring to the boil and simmer for 15 minutes or until slightly soft. Drain and cool in the sieve under cold running water.

Put the vinegar, one pint of water, sugar, clove, cinnamon, bay leaf, peppercorns and salt into the pan, bring to the boil and simmer for five minutes. Gently add the pears, bring to the boil again, then cool. Put the pears into sterilized glass jars, fill with the liquid, then screw on the lids.

GRILLED HERRINGS WITH CIDER VINEGAR SAUCE

The tangy sauce is an ideal complement to the richness of grilled herrings.

    8 herring fillets
    2 tablespoons olive oil
    3 tablespoons cider vinegar
    3 oz (75g, ⅓ cup) unsalted butter
    1 teaspoon dried dill or a small handful of fresh dill, snipped
    Black pepper

Preheat the grill.

Brush the herring fillets with oil and sprinkle with black pepper. Place on a lightly oiled baking tray and grill for 2 minutes. Turn the fillets and grill for a further 2 minutes.

Meanwhile, bring the cider vinegar to the boil in a saucepan. Keep the cider at a simmer and cut the butter into it, whisking the mixture as it melts. Whisk in the black pepper and the dill.

Put the herring fillets on warmed plates and spoon the sauce over them.

SOUSED MACKEREL

I was brought up by the sea, and my mother frequently cooked fish. This recipe was one of our favourites. Soak up and eat some of the cooking broth with mashed potato as it's very rich in calcium.

    4 mackerel, gutted, heads, tails and fins cut off, and washed
    2 onions, sliced
    2 carrots, sliced
    1 stick celery, sliced
    3 bay leaves
    Black pepper
    6fl oz (180ml, ¾ cup) cider vinegar
    Water
    Fresh parsley or dill to decorate

Put the mackerel, onions, carrots, celery, bay leaves and pepper into a shallow casserole dish. Add the cider vinegar and enough water to cover the fish. Bake in the oven at 180°C (350°F, Gas Mark 4) for 1 hour

Decorate with the parsley or dill before serving with mashed potato, peas and some of the juices from the dish.

'POT-ROAST' LAMB IN CIDER AND CIDER VINEGAR

Vinegary sauces are traditional with roast lamb and this luxury one-pot lamb dish is particularly easy.

Leg of lamb
2lb (900g) onions, peeled and quartered
20fl oz (600ml, 2½ cups) cider
4fl oz (120ml, ½ cup) cider vinegar
2 teaspoons dried thyme or 4 sprigs fresh thyme
4 garlic cloves, peeled

Preheat the oven to 170°C (325°F, Gas Mark 3).

Place the lamb in a large roasting pan and add the onions, cider, cider vinegar, thyme and garlic. Cover with aluminium foil tucked around the edges of the pan. Cook for 3 hours.

Remove the lamb and onions and rest in a warm place. Strain the liquid, return this 'gravy' to the pan and simmer on the hob for 10 minutes to thicken it. Carve the lamb and serve with the gravy, the onions and a green vegetable.

BRAISED PORK CHOPS WITH CIDER, CIDER VINEGAR, PRUNES AND APPLES

This combination of flavours is made in heaven. Serve with buttery mashed potatoes and good green cabbage.

2fl oz (60ml, ¼ cup) olive oil

4 thick pork chops, dusted with seasoned flour

8 onions, sliced

½ tsp black pepper

2 fl oz (60ml, ¼ cup) cider vinegar

2 cooking apples, or tart dessert apples, peeled, cored and cut into large chunks

6fl oz (180ml, ¾ cup) cider

4oz (100g) ready-to-eat prunes

Handful of fresh parsley, chopped

Pre-heat the oven to 150°C (300°F, Gas Mark 2).

Heat 2 tablespoons of oil in a frying pan and add the chops. Brown them on both sides and put into a baking dish or casserole. Put the remaining oil into the frying pan, add the onions and black pepper and cook for 5 minutes. Add the vinegar and apples and continue cooking, stirring frequently to prevent sticking, for a further 5 minutes. Add the cider and prunes, and cook for 5 minutes more.

Pour the sauce from the frying pan over the chops. Cover the baking dish with foil, or the casserole with a lid, and bake for 45 minutes. Sprinkle with parsley before serving.

OXTAIL STEW

This stew of succulent flavourful beef is cheap, rich in calcium and a surprise to anyone who has always thought that sirloin and fillet steak are the best cuts.

> 2fl oz (60ml, ¼ cup) olive oil
> 4oz (100g, 1 cup) plain flour
> 1 stock cube
> Black pepper
> 1 oxtail, cut into pieces, and with most but not all the fat removed
> 2 onions, sliced
> 4 cloves garlic, crushed or chopped
> 4 carrots, sliced
> 4 sticks celery, sliced
> 4 fl oz (120ml, ½ cup) cider vinegar
> Water

Pre-heat the oven to 150ºC (300ºF, Gas Mark 2).

Mix the flour, crumbled stock cube, and pepper in a large bowl.
    Heat the oil in a large heavy-bottomed casserole.
    Coat each piece of oxtail in the flour mixture and put in the pan. Stir with a wooden spoon to brown the meat on all sides. Now add the onions, garlic, carrots and celery and continue stirring over the heat for 5 minutes. Add the cider vinegar, then enough water to cover the meat. Bring to the boil, then cover the casserole, put into the oven and cook for 2½ hours, checking every hour and adding more water if necessary.

Tips for Cooks

Apples and cider vinegar can be a great help to cooks.

Apples

Cake: keep a cake fresher longer by putting it in an airtight container along with a halved apple.

Over-salted soup or casserole: add a few peeled apple chunks to soak up excess salt, then remove after 10–15 minutes.

Tomatoes: speed up the ripening of unripe tomatoes by putting them in a paper bag with one ripe apple for each three tomatoes, for a few days. The apples release ethylene gas which speeds ripening of the tomatoes.

Cider vinegar

Beans: discourage flatulence by adding a tablespoon of cider vinegar to the water when soaking dried beans.

Cheese: help prevent stored cheese hardening by wrapping it in muslin soaked in cider vinegar.

Eggs:

- Poaching: put 2 teaspoons of cider vinegar in the water to help egg whites stay better formed.

- Hard-boiling: put 1 or 2 tablespoons of cider vinegar in the water to make eggs easier to shell.

- Boiling: put 2 tablespoons of cider vinegar in the water to help prevent shells cracking.

Jellies or jellied savoury dishes: add a teaspoon of cider vinegar to the still-warm liquid to help the gelatine set.

Meat and fish: when marinating, braising, poaching or boiling meat, or poaching fish, add half a cup of cider vinegar to each cup of liquid to make the meat or fish more tender and to draw calcium from its bones.

Meringue: add a teaspoon of cider vinegar to every 2 egg whites and leave to stand for 30 seconds before whipping. This increases their stiffness and makes meringues brilliantly white.

Pancakes: if you'd like to use buttermilk but you haven't any, add a tablespoon of cider vinegar to a cup of milk and leave it for five minutes before using.

Pastry: instead of adding water to the flour-butter mixture, add flavour by adding cider vinegar, or half and half of cider vinegar and water.

Rice or pasta: put a teaspoon of cider vinegar into the water and you'll find the cooked rice or pasta is less sticky.

Salads, vegetables and fruit: washing with a cider vinegar solution may help remove certain pesticides and potentially harmful bacteria. To make the solution mix 1 part cider vinegar to 9 parts water, immerse the produce and let it soak for 5 minutes, then rinse well.

Soups, gravy or a savoury sauce: add 2 tablespoons of cider vinegar to improve the flavour.

Stock made with a chicken carcass or other bones: add a tablespoon of cider vinegar to the water to enrich the stock with calcium from the bones.

Vegetables: when boiling or steaming vegetables, add a splash of cider vinegar to the water while cooking to help the vegetables retain their colour.

CHAPTER SIX

Make Your Own Apple Juice, Cider and Cider Vinegar

Home-pressed apple juice and home-brewed cider and cider vinegar have distinctive flavours. Cloudy apple juice and cider contain tiny fragments of suspended apple pulp and because of this they are richer in pectin, phenolic acids and certain other health-promoting phytochemicals than are clear juice and cider.

When making apple juice, cider or cider vinegar, choose containers made from food-grade stainless steel or plastic, or glass. Don't ever let cut-up or crushed apples, apple juice, or cider come into contact with containers, utensils or equipment containing iron, copper or lead.

Very, very important – to avoid spoilage of juice, cider or cider vinegar by unwanted microorganisms – is to wash containers, utensils and equipment extremely thoroughly, using very hot water and no soap, then rinse well. Your kitchen and your hands should also be very clean.

Some people recommend extra cleaning with a sulphite solution (for example, made by adding Campden tablets to water); they may also add this to their fermenting cider. However, quite a few people are sensitive to sulphites. Also, the amounts of sulphite usually do not actually sterilize – so they may leave some unwanted bacteria untouched.

Apple Juice

The most important decision you'll need to make is which variety or varieties of apple to use, as this determines the proportions of sugar and acid that will be present in the juice. Dessert apples tend to be sweet. Cooking apples tend to be more acidic, or tart. Blending the two types – for example, ⅔ sweet apples to ⅓ tart apples – enables you to adjust the sweetness and acidity of the resulting juice. Cider apples are not suitable for making apple juice for drinking. Apples must be clean and have no trace of mould.

To make cloudy apple juice:

Step 1
Select the apples. They should be newly picked, firm and shiny and definitely unbruised, undamaged and rot-free. They can be of one variety, or several – three varieties, for example. Strongly flavoured dessert apples give a good flavour, especially if you add crab apples for a hint of bitterness from their high tannin content. Bittersweet and bittersharp varieties of cider apples have relatively high tannin levels too. The sweeter apples are, the more alcoholic their juice. Autumn-gathered apples tend to be sweeter than summer ones. As a rough guide, 9kg (20lb) of apples yields 4½ litres (1 gallon) of juice.

Step 2
Wash the apples in cold water.

Step 3
Cut up or crush the apples. Either cut the apples into tiny pieces that are smaller than peas, or crush (pulp, grind or mince) them using a food processor or a fruit mill or crusher (from a wine-makers' supplier). They could even be pulped by fitting a pulping attachment (a blade called a Pulpmaster) to an electric drill or crushed (very carefully) with a hammer. Crushed apple pulp is called pomace and rather than throw it away you can add it to cut-up whole apples to make apple pie.

Step 4
Press the crushed or cut-up apples. Use an apple press (bought or hired from a wine-makers' supplier) to extract the juice from the milled apples by cold-pressing. Newly pressed apple juice goes brown within a few minutes, and it is this 'tanning' that is largely responsible for the final colour of the juice.

Either drink the apple juice at once, or keep it in the fridge for 7–14 days (any longer and it will begin to ferment). The cloudiness may settle as sediment at the bottom of the bottle so, if necessary, stir or shake the juice before you drink it.

You can help prevent the natural browning of apple juice (caused by oxidation of its tannins) by adding 1g of powdered vitamin C (ascorbic acid, from a wine-makers' supplier) to each 2 litres (3½ pints) of freshly pressed juice.

Some people make large quantities of juice and preserve it by freezing, pasteurizing (which destroys some of its vitamin C), or chemical treatment. Preservation prevents microorganisms 'spoiling' (fermenting) the juice and thereby creating gases which build up pressure in capped bottles that could make them explode. Freezing is the best method for home-made apple juice.

Freezing

To freeze apple juice, pour it into plastic containers, filling them not quite full (to allow for expansion), then cover and freeze. Frozen juice keeps well for at least a year. Shake thawed juice before drinking it, as its valuable cloudiness tends to settle as sediment. Unless you pasteurized the juice (*see* below) before freezing it, keep it in the fridge after thawing.

Pasteurizing

To pasteurize apple juice, sterilize glass Kilner jars, or glass bottles that can be capped, by pouring boiling water into them and over the jar lids and bottle caps. Now fill them with the juice, leaving an inch free at the top. Put the open jars or bottles in a large pan, fill the pan with water to a level of about 5cm (2in) below the open top of the lowest jar or bottle, and heat the water to 85°C (167°F), checking with a thermometer. Simmer at this temperature for 10 minutes. This destroys the apples' natural yeasts. Remove the bottles, put them on a wooden or plastic board, and close or cap them when the bottles are cool enough to handle.

Preserving

To preserve the juice chemically, add the food preservative potassium sorbate (available as a wine stabilizer from wine-makers' suppliers; use as directed on the packet). This does not inhibit enzymes or all bacteria, though, so the flavour and colour of the juice may deteriorate after a few days, and the cloudiness may eventually settle out.

Commercial apple juice may be cloudy (unfiltered) or clear (filtered). To clarify cloudy juice, it is first left to settle overnight; the clear juice is then siphoned from the sediment (racked) then filtered. Commercial juice is usually pasteurized and may also be treated in other ways. The label may give more information.

Cider

Cider is made from apples by allowing or encouraging fermentation of natural apple sugars (and, perhaps, of added sugar) to alcohol. This is known as 'yeast' or 'alcoholic' fermentation.

Traditionally made cloudy cider is richer in health-promoting proanthocyanidin plant pigments than are many red wines – and certainly than most commercial ciders.

The two main reasons for making cider at home are that it's both cheap and easy to produce delicious cloudy cider. Another reason is that you can produce cider free from added sulphite, whereas most commercial ciders have had sulphite (or bisulphite or metabisulphite) added to help prevent spoiling. The concern is that perhaps as many as 1 per cent of us are sensitive to sulphites, and some are seriously so. Sulphite sensitivity is not a true food allergy, but its symptoms are similar. If you are buying cider and want to avoid added sulphite, read the label.

Making cider

This is how to make cloudy cider at home:

Step 1
Make apple juice. The first step is to make a batch of cloudy apple juice, as on page 110–11.

Step 2a
Either: treat the juice. Help ensure a successful brew by measuring sugar, acidity and pH. If necessary, blend in some extra juice from apples with more sugar or acidity or a lower pH.

Sugar level: In a good summer, the sugar level of apple juice may be as high as 17 per cent; in a cool wet one it may be less than 10 per cent. You can estimate the sugar content – and therefore the likely alcohol content of the finished cider – with a hydrometer, a gadget available from suppliers which measures the specific gravity ('heaviness') of the juice. For example, a specific gravity of 1.070 suggests a sugar content of 15 per cent and an eventual alcohol content of 8.5 per cent. And a specific gravity of 1.045 suggests a sugar content of 10 per cent and an eventual alcohol content of 6 per cent. If your juice has a specific gravity of less than 1.045 and you have no sweeter juice to blend with it, you may want to add sugar; if you don't, the alcohol content of the finished cider may not be high enough to prevent it spoiling. Add 12–15g of sugar to each litre of juice and stir well. Retest with the hydrometer and repeat if necessary.

Acidity and pH: An apple's acidity is determined more by its variety than by the climate. It's useful to know the acid content and pH (acid-alkaline balance) of juice. Ideally, the juice should have a malic acid content of 0.3–0.5 per cent. If it contains less, the pH will be too high and fermentation will be susceptible to bacterial infection. If it contains more, the pH will be too low and the finished cider will taste too sharp. One option is to measure the acidity with a titration kit, and measure the pH with a pH meter (both from a wine-makers' supplier). Aim for a pH of 3.2–3.8. Many bittersweet cider apples have a high pH, so need blending with more acidic fruit.

Step 2b
Or: just taste the juice! If, like many home cider-makers, you prefer not to bother with measuring sugar, acidity and pH, and are content to accept a slightly higher risk of failure, simply taste the juice:

- If it tastes insipid, and you have no other juice for blending, add malic acid in doses of 1g per litre and keep tasting until you think it tastes better.

- If it tastes too acid, and you cannot blend the sharpness out with other juice, add malic acid (in the recommended dose) to encourage malolactic fermentation, or alternatively, add calcium carbonate to neutralize the acid (in a dose of 1g per litre and repeated as necessary). Malic acid and calcium carbonate (precipitated chalk) are available from wine-makers' suppliers.

Step 3
Strain the juice. Strain the blended juice through a coarse sieve, pour it into a glass demijohn ('carboy', from a wine-makers' supplier), and put this in a cool dark place, at around 10°C (50°F) or lower.

Step 4

Let the juice ferment. Letting wild yeasts and bacteria ferment the juice can work well but may produce cider with vinegary or other unwanted flavours. Alternatively, speed up fermentation and make the result more reliable by adding wine yeast plus sugar syrup, though this may produce a somewhat bland cider.

If you decide to add yeast:

- Add wine yeast (not brewer's or baker's yeast!) from a wine-makers' supplier, according to the instructions on the packet.

- Add a teaspoon of sugar or honey per litre (2 pints) of cider.

- Consider encouraging efficient fermentation by adding yeast nutrients: add 0.2mg of thiamine and up to 300mg of ammonium salt per litre.

Fermentation usually begins within 48 hours. Early on, there is considerable bubbling caused by the release of carbon dioxide as the yeasts multiply and break down the sugar. This usually continues for about three days. When it subsides, fit an airlock (from a wine-makers' supplier) so carbon di-oxide can get out but air can't get in. You should see bubbles escaping through the airlock within two to three days; this will continue for one to three months, until all the sugar has been fermented into alcohol.

When no bubbles go through the airlock during five minutes of watching, remove the airlock and use a clean plastic tube to siphon the clear cider into another container, leaving the sediment behind. This is called racking the cider. Rinse the original container well, pour the cider back in and replace the airlock. If the airlock's 'thimble' goes back up within 24 hrs, leave the cider for a week then rack it again. Repeat the racking three times if necessary.

Step 5
Bottle and store the cider. Bottle the cider when the airlock thimble no longer comes back up within 24 hours of racking. Ideally, store bottled cider for three to six months before drinking. This improves its flavour by allowing continuing malolactic fermentation, in which malic acid is converted to lactic acid.

Cider Vinegar

Cider vinegar results from the fermentation by *acetobacter* bacteria of the sugar in cider to acetic acid. It's easier to make home-made cider vinegar than to make cider, because yeast is the only thing you'll need to add. The flavour of home-made cider vinegar is often more delicate and complex than that of the commercial sort, and because it has not been pasteurized, its flavour may continue developing over several years.

Most commercial producers convert cider to cider vinegar within a few hours by using a large fermenter with forced aeration and added *acetobacter*. Domestic cider-vinegar makers cannot buy these bacteria and most commercially produced vinegars do not work as a starter to set off and encourage fermentation, since they have been pasteurized and so contain no *acetobacter*. Wild *acetobacter* bacteria eventually find their way into cider, but adding an active starter (*see* below) aids fermentation. Use wooden, glass or food-grade stainless steel containers when making or storing cider vinegar. Do not use other metal, plastic, or glazed ceramic containers.

Making cider vinegar

Step 1
Make apple juice as on page 110–11, noting that the sweeter the apples, the stronger the cider vinegar will be.

Step 2
Consider adding brewer's yeast (according to the instructions on the packet); while not essential, this hastens alcoholic fermentation.

Step 3
Put the juice into an open container, filled only three-quarters full, to ensure easy entry of *acetobacter* bacteria, cover with a muslin cloth tied around the rim of the container to exclude insects, and leave in a warm dark place. It should start bubbling within a few days.

Step 4
Aerate the mixture each day by stirring vigorously, and keep warm at around 18–30ºC (65–86ºF). Gradually a whitish gel-like raft of 'vinegar mother' will form. This contains *acetobacter* bacteria plus the cellulose they make to keep them floating, since they need plenty of air.

Step 5
Consider speeding fermentation by adding some previously made unpasteurized and preservative-free cider vinegar. Not

only do *acetobacter* thrive in a more acidic environment, but the added vinegar will probably supply some live *acetobacter* from remaining traces of vinegar mother, and these will act as a starter. Add about 100ml (just under 4fl oz) to each litre of fermenting liquid.

Step 6
Leave the cider vinegar undisturbed for four weeks if you have added yeast, eight weeks if not, then taste it. If you think it is vinegary enough, siphon the rest into bottles, filling them to the top and capping them. If not vinegary enough, leave it for as long as it takes, tasting every week. It is better not to filter cider vinegar. And there is no need to pasteurize small quantities of home-made cider vinegar. Traces of vinegar mother may show as slight cloudiness or as gelatinous particles.

Useful Addresses and Websites

Here is a selection of the many companies and organizations concerned with apples, apple products, and cider and cider-vinegar making.

United Kingdom

Aspalls
Tel: 0044 1728 860510
www.aspall.co.uk
Makes preservative-free, unpasteurized apple juice, 'cyder' and 'cyder' vinegar.

Boots the Chemist
Larger branches carry a wide range of wine-making chemicals and sundries.

Bramley Apple Information Service
0044 20 7808 9851
www.bramleyapples.co.uk
Offers on-line recipes and information about apples, as well as recipes in a booklet and a quarterly e-letter.

Brogdale Collections
Tel: 0044 1795 536250
www.brogdalecollections.co.uk
Houses 2,300 varieties of apple tree – the largest collection
in the world. The collection is open to the public, along with
exhibitions, demonstrations, talks, day schools and workshops.

Common Ground
Tel: 0044 1747 850820
www.commonground.org.uk
Publishes information about apples and co-ordinates National
Apple Day (in October).

English Apples & Pears Limited
Tel: 0044 1795 535286 or 535462
www.englishapplesandpears.co.uk
Represents the industry and promotes English apples and
pears.

H P Bulmer Limited
Tel: 0044 1432 352000
www.bulmer.com
The world's largest maker of cider, including the Strongbow,
Woodpecker and Scrumpy Jack brands.

National Association of Cider Makers
Tel: 0044 117 3178135
www.cideruk.com
Represents cider producers and promotes the cider industry in
the UK. Has an on-line biannual newsletter, 'Cider Matters'.

www.orangepippin.com
This website for apple enthusiasts and orchardists describes
the flavours of apples and the origins of different varieties. It

also lists its own top 10 apples and the top 10 apples chosen by consumers.

Somerset Cider Vinegar Co
Tel: 0044 1278 723292
www.somersetcidervinegarco.co.uk
Uses cider apples to produce cider vinegar that is aged for 2 years.

The Brew Shop
Tel: 0044 161 480 4880
www.thebrewshop.com
Cider-makers' supplies, including apple presses for sale or hire.

The Campaign for Real Ale (CAMRA)
Tel: 0044 1727 867 201
www.camra.org.uk
CAMRA has a subgroup, The Apple and Pear Produce Liason Executive (APPLE), which aims to protect traditional English varieties of cider and perry; it also publishes the *Good Cider Guide* which lists pubs in Britain that offer real cider.

Wineworks
Tel: 0044 1246 279382
www.wineworks.co.uk/product/pulpmaster/
Cider-makers' supplies, including a Pulpmaster (a pulping blade that you fit to an electric drill) and a manual apple crusher.

Vigo Limited
Tel: 0044 1404 892101
www.vigopresses.co.uk
Cider-makers' supplies, including apple presses and crushers.

United States

Apple Products Research & Education Council
Tel: +1 404 2523663.
www.appleproducts.org
Provides information on apples and apple products.

Leeners
www.leeners.com
Tel: +1 800 543 3697
Supplies equipment for making apple juice and cider.

US Apple Association
www.usapple.org
Promotes apples and apple products and provides information
to consumers, educators, the media and industry.

USDA (United States Department of Agriculture)
www.usda.gov
Provides information on apples, apple juice, cider and cider
vinegar.

These websites provide state-specific and other information
about apples:
www.bestapples.com (Washington)
www.calapple.org
www.michiganapples.com
www.nyapplecountry.com

Australia

Apple and Pear Australia Ltd
www.apal.org.au
Represents commercial apple growers in Australia; its website
provides recipes, and health and other information about
apples.

Have an Aussie Apple
www.haveanaussieapple.com
This website is funded by Horticulture Australia Ltd and
offers consumers apple-related recipes and health and other
information.

New Zealand

Horticulture New Zealand
www.hortnz.co.nz
Represents commercial growers

Pipfruit New Zealand
www.pipfruitnz.co.nz
Tel: +64 6 873 7080
Represents the New Zealand pipfruit industry; its website
provides information, news and links to other apple-related
websites.

Other

The World Apple and Pear Association
www.wapa-association.org
Represents major apple- and pear-producing countries globally
and has a news section.

Index